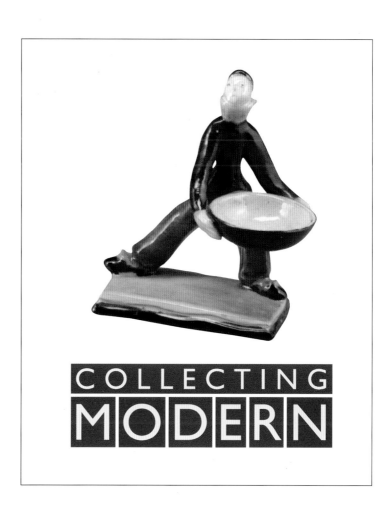

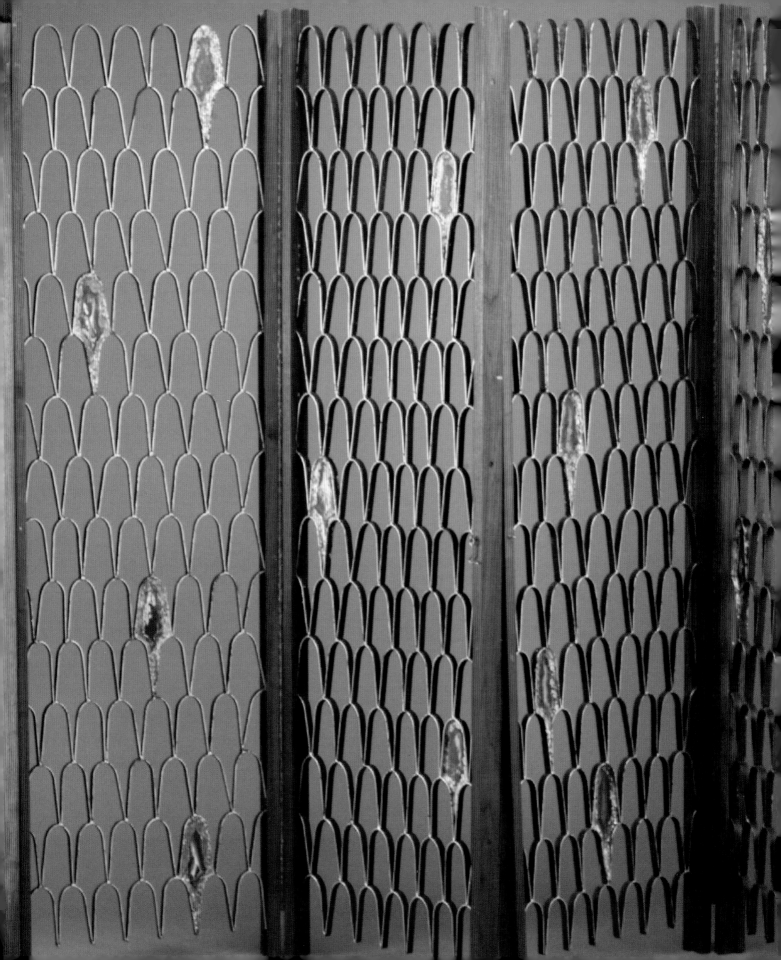

COLLECTING MODERN

A Guide to Midcentury Studio Furniture and Ceramics

David Rago
and
John Sollo

Room dividers
Paul Evans/Philip Powell

Two-panel, welded-steel room dividers on walnut frames,
with gold-washed lattice in fish-scale pattern.

GIBBS·SMITH
P
PUBLISHER

Salt Lake City

To Suzanne, Elaine, Mary Lynn, and Denise.
— DR

To Bob Miles, Calvin Dyer, and Erma Knoch.
— JS

First Edition
05 04 03 02 01   4 3 2 1

Printed in Hong Kong
Designed by Kurt Wahlner

Library of Congress Cataloging-in-Publication Data

Rago, David
   Collecting modern : a guide to midcentury studio furniture and ceramics / David Rago and John Sollo.—1st ed.
      p. cm.
      ISBN 1-58685-051-2
1. Decorative arts—Collectors and collecting—United States. 2. Decorative arts—United States—History—20th century. 3. Art pottery, American—Collectors and collecting. 4. Furniture, American—Collectors and collecting. 5. Modernism (Art)—United States. I. Sollo, John. II. Title.
NK808 .R3 2001
745'.0973'075—dc21

                                        2001003118

Bench
George Nakashima

Published by
Gibbs Smith, Publisher
PO Box 667
Layton, UT 84041

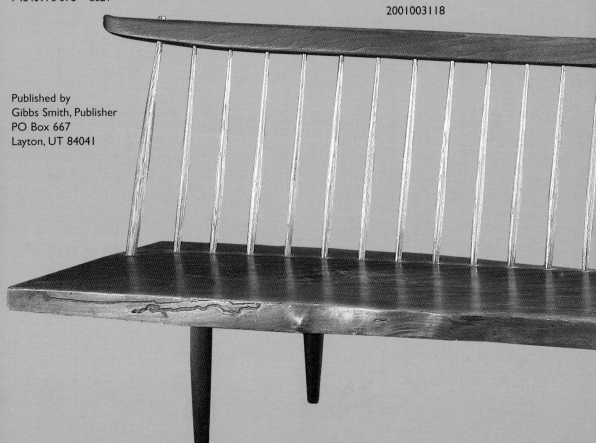

Contents

Introduction to Collecting

The fastest-growing segment of the art and collectibles market is midcentury Modern furniture and decorative arts. There are many reasons for this, including its tremendous availability, relatively low cost, and imaginative variety. But it is also true that the maturity and inquisitiveness of today's collectors have created a viable forum for things that are relatively new, in contrast to the persistent desire to value only things that are reassuringly old.

Not very long ago, it seemed that the average buyer of art and antiques needed the objects of their pursuit to be sufficiently aged to be credible. For example, the furniture of Thomas Chippendale was valued for generations by our ancestors. We were raised knowing it was special and worthy of the pedestal it rested securely upon. Louis XIV? Who could deny that prime pieces from this period were bona fide antiques? Ming Dynasty porcelain? You get the idea.

But this changed steadily during the twentieth century, beginning with Art Nouveau, Art Deco, and finally, the Arts & Crafts movement. Typical art and antiques collectors regularly turned their noses up at such notions. After all, how could something so recent be any good? It seemed that age, more than anything else, was the qualifier of merit.

Modern by David Rago

I recall vividly the annoyance expressed during the 1970s at my relatively innocent attempts to market American art pottery and Mission furniture. The established art and antiques dealers, on any given occasion, reminisced with a mixture of condescension and joy at how they used furniture by the likes of Gustav Stickley as firewood. Even the revolutionary art pottery of George Ohr was used for target practice by some of his heirs.

The first clue that this was changing became apparent when professors and schoolteachers began searching for these early-twentieth-century icons. It is a fact that from about 1965 to 1975 a disproportionate number of collectors of Art Nouveau and Arts & Crafts were educators. Overeducated and underpaid, they well knew the value of these marvelous things and could ill afford the more established works made up through the Victorian era. A good rule of thumb in ferreting out undervalued quality in design is to watch what museum curators and art historians are buying for their own collections.

Predictably, the prices for and interest in Arts & Crafts and Art Nouveau increased so rapidly during the 1970s that it was only a matter of time before they, too, outstripped the financial resources of the learned middle class. By the mid-1980s, Hollywood and Wall Street began to understand the stoic beauty (if not the philosophy) of Mission oak, and prices skyrocketed. Art Nouveau, the darling of the belle monde and drug dealers alike, had already darted for higher ground. What was an aspiring aesthete to do?

I remember my first brush with Modern material one rainy afternoon in a soon-to-be-former Arts & Crafts collector's lower Manhattan loft about 1978. Mark McDonald and Ralph Cutler were showing off some brightly colored stuff that had been made by a certain Mr. Eames not so long ago. To my undereducated eye, not long accustomed to the chunky brown simplicity of Stickley and, literally, his brothers, this seemed like a lot to ingest.

This Eames "hang it all," for example, was made of metal and wood, mixed round things with wire things, and was abundantly colorful with fragments of red, yellow, blue, and white. They assured me, though I was incapable of believing it then, that this was to be the "next big thing."

Mark and Ralph eventually opened one of the first Modern galleries in America. They soon teamed with Mark Isaacson, a visionary by anyone's standards, and moved into a grand space not far from my Manhattan studio, calling the venture Fifty-50. I remember walking through this airy showroom, amused, baffled, and intrigued by the weird colors and forms.

Another cool thing about this Modern stuff was that many of the artists who designed these pieces were either still alive or sufficiently archived so that a tremendous amount of information on them and their work was still available. I recall an exhibition, held in 1980 at Mark Isaacson's Soho Gallery, on the pottery of the Scheiers (featured on pages 46-55). In addition to a mesmerizing assortment of their ceramic and "flat art" pieces, the Scheiers themselves were in attendance. I'd never had that opportunity with the likes of such Arts & Crafts–period luminaries as the Roycrofter Elbert Hubbard and the well-traveled designer Frederick Rhead.

It would have been impossible to know then that, fifteen years later, my coauthor and I would be involved in hosting our own semiannual Modern auction series. America is a society that looks quickly for the next big thing; I call it the blue M & Ms syndrome, where our culture's short attention span causes us to become quickly bored. On a superficial level, Modern furniture and decorative arts have certainly become the next big thing.

A good rule of thumb in ferreting out undervalued quality in design is to watch what museum curators and art historians are buying.

But the interest in these things relatively new will endure for generations to come because the recent past has so much to offer. Chippendale, mentioned earlier in this introduction, was indeed a brilliant designer and craftsman. But does anyone actually believe great craftsmanship and design stopped there? The less liberal among us would have it that the Belters and Emile Galle, and maybe even Gustav Stickley and L. C. Tiffany, were equal to the challenge. But that's still an easy supposition because these important designers are long dead and their works have been validated by collectors, museums, and scores of tomes for decades. It's a lot safer to accept and admire that which a previous generation has already venerated.

And this is precisely what makes Modern material and the people who collect it so different, if not extraordinary. While a week doesn't seem to pass without some new exhibition, gallery show, or book on some obscure Modern designer or another appearing, there seems to be a certain leap of faith, or otherwise internal certitude, found among present-day collectors.

Some of the reasons for this are more personal and mundane. There are those who enjoy being around the things they grew up with. I remember the day my parents finally bought some new furniture back in 1960. Most of it was knock-off Danish Modern and the like. But there was this wood-and-metal Nelson star clock that adorned our kitchenette. It still hangs there, forty years later, keeping good time and attesting to how close our family was to at least a marginal hipness during the bleak Eisenhower years.

While the more avant-garde aspects of collecting Modern had diminished by the 1990s, there were those early buyers who reveled in how odd and unpopular such material was at that first stage. By the early 1990s, enough New York and Los Angeles dealers were developing a market base to attract the attention of mainstream publications.

As soon as the recession of the early 1990s eased, it was evident that furniture of molded wood and plastic was the next big thing.

This interest, and the fact that Modern furniture started appearing in movie sets and fashion spreads, was a clear indication that cool was coming. As soon as the recession of the early 1990s eased, it was evident that furniture of molded wood and red plastic was the next big thing.

Modern furniture was still inexpensive enough in the mid-1990s to attract a young collecting base worldwide. While there were always those who needed their furnishings accompanied by a fresh packing crate (or, in some cases, to have the joy of assembling it themselves), prices were soon irrevocably driven by an army of self-assured collectors who more than understood the fun and importance of midcentury design.

The dot-com economy of the late 1990s drove prices to the point where they doubled, and doubled again. Large furniture companies, such as Knoll, reissued premier lines that had been shelved for decades or, in many cases, simply increased the production of those that never lost the attention of the design-conscious.

We are currently in the phase of a mature market where, in search of more blue M & Ms, some new buyers are looking for the new next big thing, whatever that turns out to be. But this, perhaps more than anything else, offers a true perspective on how permanent a fixture midcentury Modern will remain. It seems that new markets, at some point, have to fall out of favor so that, upon later re-evaluation, they finally become accepted.

In my capacity as publisher of *Modernism Magazine,* I once received an anonymous letter telling me that I was selling the "emperor's new clothes." Modern masters indeed, they went on to say. This was little more than a passing trend that I was helping to fuel out of misguided ignorance and personal gain. They ended by suggesting I get a "real job."

That was one of the most validating letters I've ever received because it was a wayward shot from a dying sensibility.

In my thirty years as a decorative arts dealer, I've never experienced so broad a collecting base fueled by such self-confidence and knowledge. It has been an invaluable experience, from my puzzling introduction at the hands of Mark and Ralph to helping develop the auction market for the best the postwar period has to offer. Seldom is a dealer/auctioneer in any given field provided the opportunity to see a market grow from its very beginning to one of such broad-based respectability.

We'll review in this book the time lines leading up to and through this midcentury phenomenon. John Sollo and I have selected key artists and producers to sketch the enthusiasm and vitality of this era. We doubt that any single book could do little more than begin to describe the talents of designers and factories worldwide. This one is far from an exception. But it is our hope that we will at least spark your interest and open your mind to the possibility that the next big designer might be born tomorrow, and that many were working a scant fifty years ago.

Modern Pottery

While not often appreciated as fine art, Modern ceramics said as much about the evolution of midcentury design as any other art form. The shapes and colors, as well as the techniques employed, were all symptoms of a new and revolutionary approach to this ancient aesthetic. The studios creating the best American ware were similar to those creating Modern craft furniture. These were non-factory producers, developing their personal styles while shaping the decorative arts.

The significance of Modern ceramic design is best understood against a backdrop of the stylistic evolution of decorative ceramics in America. While the more contemporary pieces are stimulating in their own right, they take on a richer context when the foundation established for them by their predecessors is examined.

After reviewing this design evolution, we'll look at several key Modern potters: Edwin and Mary Scheier, Otto and Gertrud Natzler, Peter Voulkos, Rose Cabat, and Maija Grotell. These were chosen not necessarily for the prominence

Bowl
Edwin and Mary Scheier

Photo courtesy Gansevoort
Gallery, New York.

ROSEVILLE

Vases from the Roseville Pottery, Zanesville, Ohio. These examples of rare Roseville artist-decorated lines date to about 1906. While the forms were cast and the designs were offered through catalogs, they are, nevertheless, products of a single artist decorating each piece. The lower vase, a Sunflower-pattern *jardiniere*, dates to 1930. One of their more popular production lines, the decoration was embossed in the mold and an "artist" applied the appropriate colors. The screened photos opposite are Roseville pottery production ware, ca. 1940.

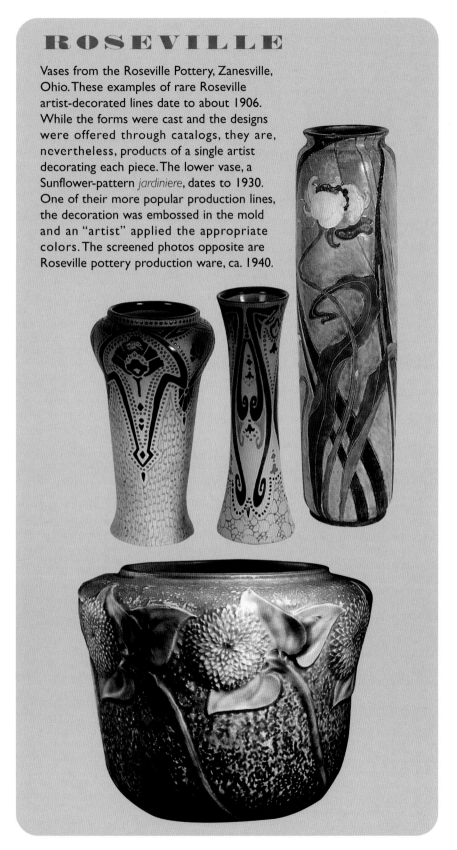

of their work. Peter Voulkos, for example, remains to this day an extraordinary potter of immeasurable influence, while Rose Cabat was a relatively little-known potter who quietly pursued her craft on the fringes. Rather, these artists produced bodies of work that dovetail neatly into one another, in spite of how vastly different each of them and their work was. We'll focus on a thirty-year period, during which time their work overlapped, and consider how personal and extravagantly different the ceramic arts had become.

For all intents and purposes, art pottery in the United States began with the Centennial Exposition in Philadelphia in 1876. While there had been some dabbling and experimentation with decorative ware prior to that time, such as at the Chelsea Keramic Art Works in Chelsea, Massachusetts, most of what came before had focused on more traditional decorated porcelain.

The need for utilitarian, if not decorative, pottery and porcelain in the United States was met mostly by imports. Nearly all of the finest ware was imported from Europe and the Orient, with only an occasional brilliant effort from key American producers.

It wasn't so much that America couldn't produce a suitable ware. Factories such as Tucker Porcelain in Philadelphia, Pennsylvania, and Ott and Brewer in Trenton, New Jersey, were certainly up to the task. But America at this time was at once desirous of foreign luxury goods and, by any measure, a young country. In Germany, for example, companies such as the Meissen Works had been producing extraordinary porcelain since the early eighteenth century, and in England, the porcelain industry was of equal age and stature. How daunting it must have been for American producers to even attempt art porcelain. And, in a country still exploring and expanding its borders, an upwardly mobile middle class was just beginning to form in the wake of the Industrial Revolution and the Civil War. It wasn't until after the Civil War and Reconstruction that American households became increasingly interested in decorative ware.

The Centennial Exposition in 1876 hastened this artistic shift. In many ways, this international fair embarrassed American artists by illustrating so clearly the aesthetic chasm between them and the European manufacturers they had so often emulated. It didn't seem to matter much that the British, French, and Germans had a century or more head start to develop their industries. Instead, the leading proponents of this nascent field, with tails collectively between their legs, scrambled back to their respective centers to improve their craft.

The influence and importance of European predecessors were undeniable. While the fledgling American industry was a marvel of the country's ingenuity and drive, they more often than not imported European masters to further the cause. In Trenton, New Jersey, for example, two masters from County Cork, Ireland, were imported to develop the eggshell-thin Belleek, made famous in their homeland (and which exists to this day as a thriving product).

Cincinnati, Ohio, was one of the hotbeds of ceramic design, largely due to the china-painting craze that swept through the Queen City and the efforts of a handful of industrious women and men under the tutelage of Englishman Ben Pittman. As might be expected, these early ceramic decorators created their share of poorly decorated china.

ROOKWOOD

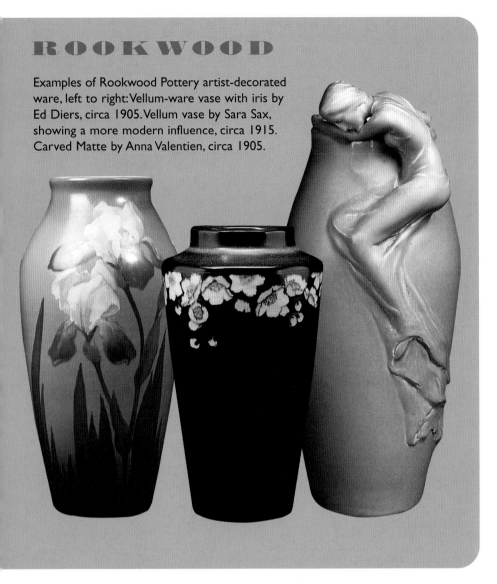

Examples of Rookwood Pottery artist-decorated ware, left to right: Vellum-ware vase with iris by Ed Diers, circa 1905. Vellum vase by Sara Sax, showing a more modern influence, circa 1915. Carved Matte by Anna Valentien, circa 1905.

But they had to start somewhere.

They could do little more by 1880 than adopt decorative styles and techniques already popularized by Europeans and people of the ancient Orient. Haviland Pottery of Limoges, France, successfully created an underglaze-decorated ware characterized by painted subjects, mostly flowers, in thick slip relief on blended backgrounds, mostly blue. The earlier work in Cincinnati—pieces by Louise McLaughlin, Thomas Wheatley, and the firm of Rettig and Valentine— nicely approximated these but did little to improve the overall quality of the ware.

Another Cincinnati luminary, Maria Longworth Nichols, founded the world-famous Rookwood Pottery in 1880, which was to be a turning point for American ceramics. While their earliest work was equally derivative and similarly unsatisfactory, this was a company with a longer vision and strong legs. By the mid-1880s, they used experimentation, keen management, and the best ceramic artists in America to build a qualitative product with an eye to changing styles and taste.

Though slogging through a mostly unimpressive Victorian period, when Rookwood's copies of European copies of Japanese and Chinese art ware became their main product, they lurched into the 1890s almost anticipating the curvilinear lines and florid sensibilities of Art Nouveau. While they maintained their primary Victorian ware—Standard Brown glaze (a brown overglaze that darkened the colors of the slip-relief decoration)—they adopted the friendlier hues of three new lines: Aerial Blue, Sea Green, and Iris (respectively blue, green, and clear overglazes layered above pastel-shaded grounds).

With another addition, Vellum Ware, they embraced the work of the Impressionists. This new glaze, with a gauze-like diffusion of the decoration, often cloaked stylized landscapes with a very modern, and vastly different, appeal. All this change occurred in a mere twenty-year period, readying Rookwood to win a Gold Medal in the Paris Exposition Universelle in 1900. The embarrassment of the Centennial Exposition twenty-four years earlier had indeed contributed to dramatic change in the decorative arts in America.

FULPER

While the Fulper Pottery, of Flemington, New Jersey, worked in the nineteenth century as producers of salt-glazed utilitarian stoneware, they began to market art pottery about 1909. These are early (1910–15) art pieces showing an expressive Oriental style.

Victorian sensibilities turned first to Art Nouveau and then to Arts & Crafts. While the former style used the ceramic vessel as a surface on which to paint, the latter treated it as part of a whole. Because most of the hand-painted ceramics were made in the Ohio Valley (mainly Cincinnati and Zanesville), we refer to this as the Ohio school. The Art Nouveau style of ceramics was largely centered there.

The Arts & Crafts style, however, was more loosely translated by artisans across the nation, first on the East Coast and in the South, and later in California. Unlike the Ohio school, which relied upon larger factories with a division of labor, the Arts & Crafts artists were decidedly more hands-on, either operating their own studios or decorating in smaller factories with more of a connection between them and the finished product.

Arts & Crafts at once expressed America's dependence on European precedents as well as its slow turn away from them. It would be unfair to say that Victorian ceramics in America were derivative from European precedents and that Arts & Crafts ceramics weren't. William Grueby of Boston,

MARBLEHEAD

Marblehead Pottery, of Marblehead, Massachusetts, was an Arts & Crafts producer of the highest order. Each of these pieces was hand thrown and individually decorated (and often signed) by an artist. Marblehead's small studio also produced enamel-glazed, hand-thrown "undecorated" ware, but multicolor pieces remain a collector favorite. These vases date from around 1910–15.

GRUEBY

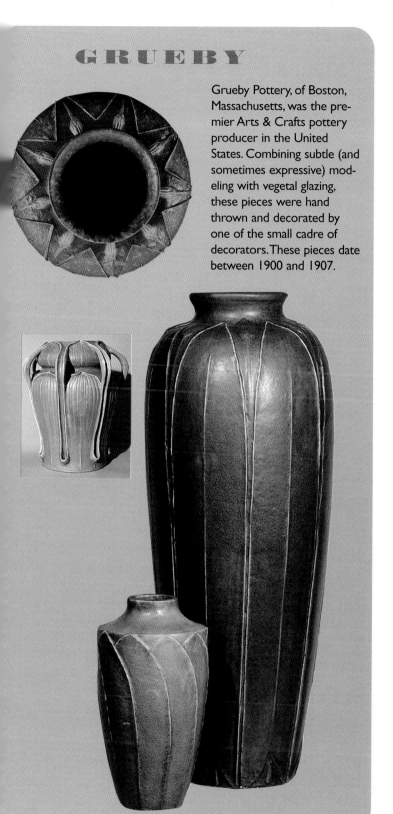

Grueby Pottery, of Boston, Massachusetts, was the premier Arts & Crafts pottery producer in the United States. Combining subtle (and sometimes expressive) modeling with vegetal glazing, these pieces were hand thrown and decorated by one of the small cadre of decorators. These pieces date between 1900 and 1907.

Massachusetts, for example, freely copied forms and design ideas from the French ceramics master Auguste Delaherche.

Nevertheless, the Arts & Crafts practitioners sought to do more than simply replicate what came before. "Adopt, adapt, and adept" was more in keeping with this twentieth-century American spirit. Grueby, though emulating Delaherche, added to the Frenchman's inspiration a series of opaque enamel glazes imitating the natural, vegetal skins of gourds and squash.

This was also a time when new decorative techniques were being introduced into American craft and, in some cases, to the world. Grueby, whose ceramics are still regarded as among the most important of the twentieth century, imported the deep modeling and sculpting of the ceramic form from Europe. His idiosyncratic contemporary, George Ohr, from Biloxi, Mississippi, developed a wholly new range of manipulative dialogue, ripping, crimping, pinching, and otherwise prodding the vessel into a vastly different realm. In the process, Ohr redefined the ceramic craft as one that didn't necessarily have to translate to pretty vases, or to vases at all, for that matter. Instead, the vessel form was something that could simply define space.

O H R

George Ohr's pottery pushed the envelope years before such experimentation became acceptable in the U.S. His aggressively decorated ware was met mostly with derision until the 1970s. These are circa 1900.

In fact, the evolution of ceramic design can be traced by observing the decorative techniques employed by the potters. Earlier works were mostly painted in slip, or powdered clay mixed with pigments, that fused with the vessel wall during firing. Modeling and carving the ceramic surface were used only in minor ways before the influences of the Arts & Crafts period were more widely adopted. During the Arts & Crafts period, from about 1900 to 1915, sculpting and modeling the ceramic surface became favored decorative techniques. Unlike slip-painting over the pot's surface, hand-tooling integrated the design and the vessel, creating a more unified product.

Around the time of World War I, molded designs became more prevalent as America moved toward commercial ware. At this time, the cost of materials became less dear than the cost of labor, and hand-decorated ware—at least the sort produced in factories—soon began to price itself out of the market.

Ceramic sculpture, though used in limited ways in the United States since the Victorian era, became very popular and more widespread during the Great Depression. This seems largely the case because of the influx of European potters and the art they had practiced in places like Austria and Germany. Potters/teachers such as Vally Wieselthier and Maija Grotell, who will be discussed later in this chapter, were among such luminaries who brought these and other ideas to the West in the decades after World War I.

Beginnings of the Studio Movement

World War I was a defining time, bringing to an end much of the art-pottery movement. Obviously, the world then had much more on its mind than decorative art and interior design. This time saw the deterioration of factory-based art ware, the introduction of mass-produced commercial ware, and the first stirrings of the studio movement. The studio movement was more a one-on-one approach to ceramic design, involving the atelier of accomplished artists, the curriculum of major colleges, and the focus of several artist colonies across the country. The first decade after World War I was one during which the quality of ceramic arts moved both forward, in design elements and technical mastery, and backward, as the production and commercial-quality work of the factories became slicker and more repetitive.

NEWCOMB COLLEGE

Newcomb College ware was some of America's best Arts & Crafts pottery. Decorated by teachers and students from the Sophie Newcomb Memorial College (Tulane University), each piece was hand thrown and individually decorated. Glossy pieces ca. 1900–10; matte-glazed ware ca. 1910–30.

BINNS

Charles Fergus Binns was one of the most influential teachers of the ceramic arts in America from about 1905 until the depression. Though the formality of his work would ultimately prove too restrictive for American ceramists, his grasp of fundamental skills and capacity to teach them to his students was a critical part of this country's development. These pieces circa 1925.

Artists of various media fled Europe for America during the 1920s and 1930s as fascist regimes grew in power and influence. The Americanization of these European masters, formally trained and radically inspired, introduced new styles and decorative techniques. It was at this time that a Modern American style was clearly developing, in response to the lingering traditions that threatened to strangle it. On one hand, American ceramists were ennobled by the teachings of masters like Charles Fergus Binns, at Alfred University in Alfred, New York. On the other hand, his old-school methods and formal tendencies restricted the forward thinking that was necessary for a more modern approach to the craft.

It was also at this time that American factories such as Rookwood and Cowan attempted to maintain the production of respectable art ware on a larger scale, focusing more on commercial ware of excellent quality and design, but less

Cowan pottery's famous "Jazz Bowl" was designed in 1929.

on ware produced by the artist's hand. Pieces were mostly cast, and designs were becoming mostly in mold rather than hand-tooled.

There were certainly exceptions, as both companies created some of their most memorable pieces during this time. Cowan's famous "Jazz Bowl," designed in 1929 by Viktor Schreckengost (American, but trained in Austria at the Kunstgewerbeschule) is one such example. But these were, more often than not, stellar works that served to maintain the fame of the companies rather than accurately represent their current production standards.

At this time, key teachers were responsible for changing the face of the ceramic arts in America. Maija Grotell emigrated from Helsinki, Finland, in 1927 before emerging as a teacher of great influence. Glen Lukens, born in America, was a master of subtlety and craft, teaching in southern California for more than thirty years. And Vally Wieselthier, an Austrian artist who studied at the Kunstgewerbeschule under Michael Powolny and potted under Joseph Hoffmann at the Wiener Werkstatte, brought with her the vigorous designs and vibrant colors of Austrian aesthetic.

In many ways, America emerged from World War II a very different place, and no less so in the decorative arts. Between the great wars, American ceramists seemed caught in the struggle between old-school formality and the liberal aesthetic of a new world order. The Second World War served to separate the world from so much of its past, and we can see in America how this freed artists from the more traditional roots in the ceramic arts.

The rest of this section focuses on five artists who, through their efforts and influence, brought American ceramics from adolescence to adulthood. It is worth repeating that, while these artists alone cannot fully define Modern American studio ceramics, their combined efforts were responsible for elevating the field to its current world-leading status.

LUKENS & WOOD

The low bowl is by Glen Lukens, with an active green-and-white flambé ending unevenly on a clay foot, circa 1940. This bowl is typical of the subtle style of the naturalistic potting that Lukens introduced to his students in California. The pink bowl is by Beatrice Wood.

WIENER WERKSTATTE

Examples of work from the Wiener Werkstatte and other Austrian potteries from the 1920s, showing the sculptural techniques and flamboyant colors first popularized there. Vally Wieselthier, who worked under Joseph Hoffman, was one of the potters most responsible for introducing such work to American ceramists.

A grouping of Grotell pieces from her Cranbrook period, showing a variety of glazes and forms.

Maija Grotell

Maija Grotell was not only an exceptional potter but an important instructor as well. In this capacity, she bridged her European past and her American future, serving as a living metaphor of what decorative ceramics in the United States were to become.

The more one studies midcentury ceramics, the more interrelated the players in the field appear. Unlike sculpture or painting, which were far more established and recognized as valid art forms, the potting community was relatively small. In spite of the great physical distances that separated bastions of the ceramic arts, such as the Cranbrook Institute in Detroit, the Otis Institute in Los Angeles, the Henry Street Settlement House in New York City, and the Archie Bray Foundation in Helena, Montana, there was an acute awareness among ceramists of each other's work.

There was an almost familial bond in the ceramic arts that is only touched upon in this book. Vally Wieselthier, for example, learned her skills at the Wiener Werkstatte in Vienna and then immigrated to the United States to work and teach. While her stylistic influences were noteworthy, her work as a teacher was equally as important. For example, as an instructor she introduced Erni Cabat and, through him, Rose Cabat to potting. Work by Wieselthier was exhibited alongside that of many of her contemporaries, including Maija Grotell.

Grotell, in turn, was not only influential in teaching some of our most important midcentury potters while at the Cranbrook Institute, but she also hosted shows that included examples by rising stars such as Peter Voulkos who were trained elsewhere. It seems, in this regard at least, that the diminutive nature of the nascent community served its constituents well as it allowed for a cross-pollination of ideas and a mutually supportive structure when it was so greatly needed. Formal decorative ceramics in the United States was then at a crucial juncture in its seventy-five-year development, because it was finally breaking away from its European roots. There is at least some irony that it demanded the instruction and genius of European potters to finally free itself from them.

Maija Grotell was born in Helsinki, Finland, in 1899; there she studied sculpture, painting, and design at the School of Industrial Art. Her post-graduate work focused on ceramics, and she studied under one of Europe's most important artist-potters, Alfred William Finch. She immigrated to the United States in 1927, and began her work as a teacher at the Henry Street Settlement House in 1928, where she remained as an instructor until 1938. It is important to note, however, that while she made her services available at Henry Street for a decade, she concurrently instructed at other studios and schools, including Rutgers University School of Ceramic Engineering in New Brunswick, New Jersey.

Having prepared for years, Grotell finally achieved the position of head of the ceramics department at the famous Cranbrook Institute in 1938. While the powers that be would have preferred that a male head the department, it is likely that Eliel Saarinen, who was a guiding force at Cranbrook and also a Finn, played a key role in her consideration. That women potters were at a disadvantage because of their sex would soon change, in no small part because of Grotell's unique contributions.

Two Cranbrook-era pots both have active glazing and tooled geometric decorations that reinforce the angularity of the forms. Photo courtesy of Gansevoort Gallery, New York.

Opposite: A large tapering vessel with expressed horizontal throwing ridges and geometric silver decoration on a rich blue ground. Photo courtesy of Gansevoort Gallery, New York.

An earlier Grotell vessel, pregnant in form, with moon-like decoration echoing the feminine qualities of the pot. Note the soft, slightly iridescent glazing. Photo courtesy of Gansevoort Gallery, New York; photo by Eva Heyd.

When she arrived at Cranbrook, it soon became apparent that Grotell's superior potting skills were the least of what she had to offer. Reports from former students consistently describe her capacity to instruct nonverbally; this is critical in an art form that must be developed from within. Grotell conveyed much to her students as they watched her raise large yet subtly powerful forms with hands that seemed oversized for her body.

Grotell's teaching style was similar to Peter Voulkos's in that a certain informality reigned. Inviting students and faculty to address her as Maija, this seemingly small token of familiarity spoke volumes of what education in the arts was to become, particularly in the wake of World War II. Grotell was credited with changing the focus of ceramics at Cranbrook from a sculptural to a holloware aesthetic.

Her success as a teacher was apparent in another, perhaps more important way: she understood the art enough to not need her students to follow in her stylistic footsteps. Rather, she encouraged them to find an idea, a quiet place within themselves, and allow it to manifest in a way that was appropriate for them. Even if she didn't agree with a particular idea or form, if she sensed it was true to the pupil, she encouraged it nonetheless.

Grotell's work in the United States is often easy to date, not only because of the clear stylistic changes her decorative elements and techniques underwent, but also because much of it was marked in ways peculiar to specific locations. Her earliest work in America—at the Henry Street Settlement House—is extremely rare, and only a few marked pieces also bearing her signature have surfaced.

Even in works from this early period, however, her hand is unmistakable. The forms, simple but strong, show the marks of an accomplished and precise thrower. The decoration, in a simple Art Deco-influenced style, is not dissimilar to the silver-on-emerald designs of Gustavsberg's Argenta ware from Sweden, made at around the same time. One such Henry Street piece shows decoration of silver crescent moons on a soft, pastel green ground, painted on a precisely thrown flaring vase with gentle finger ridges left on the exterior. Others depict slightly abstracted forms. For example, her drawing skills were said to have a

Matisse-like flair, with colorful portraits simply yet strikingly rendered. Several other early pieces bear stylized skyscrapers and city scenes that were popular Art Deco–period motifs.

Grotell's work at Rutgers University has also proven elusive due to the fact that she was there more as an instructor than potter. Small groupings of this work occasionally surface and tend to be on a smaller scale, often bereft of decoration, but still possessing the delicately powerful quality that remained consistent throughout her career.

Toshiko Takaezu

A large, garden-sized moonpot glazed in earth tones by Toshiko Takaezu (ca. 1960).

Once Grotell arrived at Cranbrook, however, her decorative style changed more dramatically than at any time previous since she landed on American soil. The heady environment of the place, coupled with the large kiln and state-of-the-art facility, were certainly factors. It also seems likely that the recognition implicit in the position as head of the ceramics department encouraged her immeasurably.

Without changing her form selection, Grotell's personal work while in Detroit evolved in at least two ways: through glaze experimentation and decorative technique. Similar to all the potters featured in this book, Grotell continually strove to develop radically new glaze formulae. She and her students combined what was known through earlier teachings with what they discovered through trial and error, redefining old glazes and creating new ones in the process. For example, Grotell developed a volcanic-textured surface like Otto Natzler did.

Her decorative themes also continued to evolve, as representational themes became increasingly abstract. Just as American ceramists were increasingly less bound to the formal traditions of their nineteenth-century roots, decorative elements had less and less to do with mere decoration. Instead—and this is as true on Grotell's postwar work as on any pottery produced in the United States—elements of design were intended to enforce the inner theme of the work itself. This idea was accomplished through the use of gestures and linear cuts that at once defined the form of the vessel and controlled the flow of the glazes covering it. Grotell's vases in and of themselves were powerful in form, but the addition of incisions, lines, and gashes strengthened their overall appeal.

Grotell remained at the Cranbrook Institute until her retirement in 1966, at age sixty-seven. Some of America's most successful and influential potters flourished under her tutelage. Toshiko Takaezu, Richard Devore, and John Glick, all of whom became significant potters and/or teachers in their own right, are among the many who benefited from her supervision. Takaezu's work, for example, often centers on ovoid vessels with nipple openings. The forms are powerful and simple, the glazing suggesting an earthy fertility. Takaezu later went on to teach ceramics at Princeton University in Princeton, New Jersey.

The market for Grotell's decorated work has remained strong for more than two decades. This can be attributed to the innovation and quality of the work, its rarity, and her importance as a potter and

Richard Devore

Devore was a student of Grotell's at Cranbrook. His work is consistently glazed with a desert-like surface and finished with irregular edges. This shallow bowl with a depressed center (ca. 1980) is most unusual.

teacher. It is interesting to note that even her simplest work is well crafted and collectible. But the bulk of collector interest centers on larger pieces from her Cranbrook period, decorated in her trademark manner and covered with several of her bright, complementary glazes.

Advanced collectors often seek out earlier, germinal Grotell pieces from the pre-Cranbrook period. These are subtler still and appeal to a more discerning and educated eye. Henry Street pieces of any sort are desirable, though ware decorated in the Art Deco style would be at the top of any serious buyer's list. Rutgers pieces, which tend to be small and rarely appear with decoration, are also eagerly sought by collectors. A large decorated piece from this school would challenge any price ever paid for her work.

This tall vase (22 1/4 inches) by Grotell wears a turquoise glaze. Photo courtesy of Gansevoort Gallery, New York; photo by Eva Heyd.

Opposite: An exceptional and technically perfect vase from Grotell's mature period, possessing a powerful form, dynamic glazing, and stark linear decoration. Photo courtesy of Gansevoort Gallery, New York.

The Natzlers

The husband-and-wife team of Gertrud and Otto Natzler created some of the most beautiful pottery produced during the Modern movement. Their flight to America in 1938, and the subsequent success of their work here, was much in keeping with the evolution of the ceramic arts. The period after the Great Depression was, to a large extent, directed by potters either trained in Europe or who emigrated from there.

Gertrud Amon and Otto Natzler first met in Vienna, Austria, in 1933 and shortly afterward began working together in a small studio. Even from the start, they enjoyed a surprising level of commercial success, with no fewer than three outlets representing their ware.

They were graduates of different disciplines, completing their courses prior to the Great Depression. Gertrud studied at Austria's Handelsakademie, a commercial school, graduating in 1926, and Otto worked for Bundeslehranstalt fur Textil-industrie in textile design until a year later.

It was clear from the very beginning that Gertrud was a master of the throwing wheel. She had the capacity to produce paper-light forms whose strength was an illusion created from the thinnest of walls. She developed her skills further under the tutelage of Franz Iskra, a Viennese studio ceramist and teacher. It was from Gertrud that Otto first became interested in ceramic design.

In Otto's words,

> To watch Gertrud's throwing is the sensual/aesthetic experience that one has in the presence of anyone who is a master of his medium. There is the graceful movement of her hands, exerting complete positive control over the clay from the first firm grip during the centering, leading into a progressively lighter touch while

Fine Natzler footed bowl covered in a celadon and umber flambé glaze.

shaping the general outline. There is never any sign of excessive force or strained effort; it is all a continuous, completely natural, controlled motion, gradually diminishing in force, until that very last breathing of her fingertips, producing that last sensitive flare of the lip to complete and balance a form. By that time the walls of the vessel often are eggshell-thin and it seems quite incomprehensible that the soft clay can support all that weight.*

Otto soon joined Gertrud at the Iskra studio but intuitively recognized that he would never equal her throwing

The large closed bottle (11 inches tall) has an unusual orange flambé over a roughly textured surface. The form, glazing, and surface treatment are all very rare in the Natzlers' work.

skills. He gravitated to experimentation with glazing, eventually matching Gertrud's achievements in a different but marvelously compatible way. They remained with Iskra until 1935 before leaving to form a studio of their own.

In contrast to prevailing sensibilities, the Natzlers produced a relatively simple body of work. Rather than decorating their ware with tooled and/or painted designs, they chose to craft delicate vessels of perfect proportion adorned only with Otto's sensational glazes. One need only look at the work done by their Viennese contemporaries to understand how vastly different their work was. Otto himself was clear in his feelings towards this other popular ware:

> The word ceramics made me shudder. For some reason I did not relate clay with ceramics. In fact, ceramics to me meant

*Gertrud and Otto Natzler Ceramics: Catalog of the Collection of Mrs. Leonard M. Sperry, Los Angeles County Museum of Arts, 1968.

all those cute little multicolored figurines, vases, and compotes with appliquéd flowers, birds, or fruit, plates and dishes decorated with leaves or insects, clowns or mermaids, or at best, the stuff that came out of the Wiener Werkstatte, 'Angewandte Kunst' (applied art), where the little painted animal figures could be used to stamp out a cigarette in a matching ashtray. These were the ceramics I knew. I found them rather meaningless, quite distressing.[1]

Potters from the Kunstgewerbeschule, studying under Michael Powolny, were deeply influenced by the Viennese Secessionists. Flourishing between the Great Wars, such pieces were painted and modeled with bright geometric designs or sculpted with figural motifs. Famous artists like Susi Singer and Vally Wieselthier championed this expressive style. The Natzlers' work was refreshingly different and the overall quality finer and more classical.

While there seems to be no clear reference to the influence of Oriental craftsmen, the Natzlers' work was very Eastern in its approach. The idea of turning a pot on a wheel, capturing the subtleties that arise from a supreme connection to the moment, can be the only explanation for Gertrud's capacity to stand out from the thousands of potters worldwide throwing similar balls of clay on similar wheels at the same time.

Earthenware vase with a crater glaze by Gertrud and Otto Natzler. Photo courtesy of Gansevoort Gallery, New York.

Otto continued in his glaze development, creating dozens of striking colors and textures. Like most potters, he seems to have learned at least as much from his mistakes, with each "problem" pot offering a window into new ideas. He was more a technician than an artist, assiduously noting the materials he used, what he did with the kiln, and what resulted from the mix.

The first kiln firing in their new studio was a case in point. Containing "many months of work," they had little idea how to successfully bake their ware. In short, the entire contents of the kiln were overfired to a muddy brown. The one exception, a pot on a lower shelf with marvelous color, stuck to the kiln floor and was shattered when they attempted to remove it. Nevertheless, Otto took note of the part of the vase that was successful and this was factored into subsequent firings with increasing success.

Otto's glazing was important in several ways. First, his range included coatings with snowflake crystals, "melt fissures," volcanic textures, metallic lusters, and deep, vibrant monochromes. In the book *Gertrud and Otto Natzler Ceramics,*[1] which showcases the collection of Mrs. Leonard M. Sperry, he lists some of his glazes in the following way:

Pompeian (circa 1939) Glazes with fairly high lead content, thickly applied in several layers. Many show deviations from the customary glaze surface, with pockmarks, blisters, and shriveled patterns with the glaze flowing thickly in heavy folds. These are opaque, like many of my early glazes.

Lava (circa 1940) These fall into three groups of variations: lava, glowing lava, and lava stone. They are either semi-lead or pure alkaline. The lava-like surface is achieved by the addition of a titanium-silicon carbide combination to the basic glaze. The application is always thick, in several layers. In the flowing lava glazes, a light-melting overflow is used of either a related glaze or one of completely different composition. Finally, the lava stone glazes are characterized by their rough, porous texture.

Reduction (circa 1942) In the reduction process, oxygen is repeatedly eliminated from the kiln at strategic intervals during the firing cycle. The purpose is to cause color changes in the clay and glazes through the withdrawal of oxygen. Depending on the method of reduction and the material composition of the reducing agent, there can be other physical side effects in addition to the color transmutation of the glaze, in addition to smoke and flame marks. Results achieved by us prior to 1947 were frequently purely accidental.

Some of the side effects of reduction included:

● melt fissures, resulting from cooling drafts that caused the surface skin of the glaze to solidify when fired. This would leave seams in the glaze that exposed the subordinate glazing beneath.

● crater glazes that, according to Natzler, were similar in composition if not appearance to the Pompeian glazes that preceded them. They are typified by deep craters in the glaze surface.

● crystalline glazes, at least the better ones, developed about 1959. The basic principle was to produce an oversaturated solution during the firing, which, while cooling, forms crystals of the dissolved solids. Most of their crystalline glazes were transparent or semitransparent.

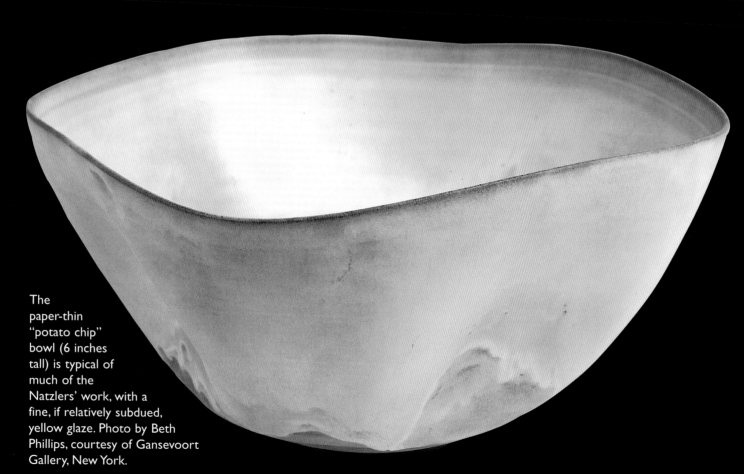

The paper-thin "potato chip" bowl (6 inches tall) is typical of much of the Natzlers' work, with a fine, if relatively subdued, yellow glaze. Photo by Beth Phillips, courtesy of Gansevoort Gallery, New York.

iridescence, which occurs when reduction is continued into the cooling cycle. This was a tricky proposition because too little would fail to have the desired effect on the metallic compounds in the glazes, and too much would turn the iridescence into what Natzler considered a "vulgar" metallic luster.

His volcanic finishes are among those most favored by contemporary collectors. They are certainly the least subtle of his work, with pock-marked surfaces in hues of cream, brown, sky blue, and green being the most common. Unlike the work of imitators who would soon follow, Otto's finishes had a controlled elegance to them, where the texture was part of the product rather than the only source of beauty.

This, more than anything, demonstrates the importance of Gertrud and Otto's collaboration. And part of the mystery of their work is how a potter so subtle and a glaze technician so demonstrative could come together, time and again, staying out of each other's way.

A study of their work over three decades reveals what may seem to the untrained eye as minimal evolution. Perhaps this is because they worked at so high a level early on. But closer scrutiny allows for a greater understanding of their achievements. More obvious are the larger, more complicated forms Gertrud produced during the late 1950s and early '60s. While the open bowl form seems a leitmotif throughout her tenure, her development of large vase- and bottle-shaped vessels marks a significant departure in her work. Otto's glazes,

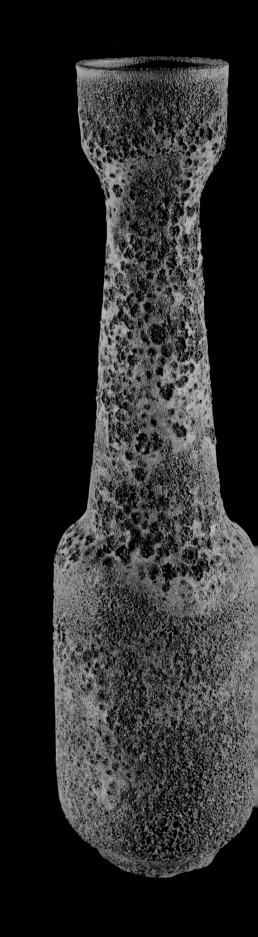

Gertrud and Otto Natzler created this earthenware bottle with crater glaze in the 1950s. Photo courtesy of Gansevoort Gallery, New York.

though not necessarily better, became more varied with the use of reduction firing and the addition of new glaze formulae.

Otto Natzler characterized Gertrud's forms in four ways. This material is outlined in the book that accompanied the Sperry Exhibition. As the work has been long out of print, and since no more succinct explanation of Gertrud's throwing exists, it is paraphrased here.

● . . . round bowl rising from a narrow base, it changes into a progressively convex curve and ends with a slight suggestion of turning back into itself. The visual center of gravity will be in the center of the pot.

● . . . bowl with flaring lip begins like a round bowl but turns outward to form the lip. There is an airiness to this form, as though floating in space, and the visual center of gravity lies in the uppermost part of the pot.

● . . . double-curve form, which can be a bowl or a bottle depending on the shape, the visual center of gravity can be in the upper or lower portion of the pot. This form is most elusive as to the arrangements of its curves and proportions. Ideally, it gives the impression of expanding and contracting motion, as if breathing.

● . . . teardrop bottle, which Otto claimed had hundreds of variations, all of which widen quickly after lifting from the base. The form ascends slowly, with a slight curve, as though turning into itself, changing direction just before ending, at times with a distinct flare. The visual center of gravity remains close to the base.[1]

Contemporary collectors seem to treasure all but the Natzlers' simplest work, these being mostly smallish bowls with basic apple green or metallic yellow finishes. Even some of Gertrud's smaller pots possess a crisp silhouette that fits neatly into period interiors. Her masterworks, however, have and will continue to set the standard in the collecting market. Because of the preponderance of bowls, nearly any vase form stands out as a superior example. And larger bottle vessels and tall vases seemed even to the Natzlers to be of special importance when they made them. Some of the most rare and interesting combinations of form and glazing can be viewed on such examples.

It is interesting to note that, throughout the tumultuous decades before and after World War II, they adhered to the same design aesthetic with which they began while the world around them changed. The influence of Danish design and an encroaching oriental aesthetic in the West seems clearly anticipated by the Natzlers' work. Less became increasingly more, and the Natzlers' bold but simple statements, consistent in craft and chemistry, eventually generated interest and enthusiasm in the collecting community.

When the Natzlers began their careers, they sought to avoid the influence of other potters and their craft. This may have been intuitive, egocentric, or both. But this self-imposed isolation allowed them to chart their own course, fueled by their love for each other. In the process, it enabled them to consistently create a fine art ware that was not dictated by the passing whim of a given day or the mercantile concerns that governed so much of popular culture.

Gertrud died young in 1971, bringing to an end this collaboration. Otto stopped potting for a while, then continued his efforts making his own ware as foils for his glazing. While the quality of his finishes never wavered, his hand-built vessels were masculine and heavy. They constitute a high level of skill, but never quite matched the elegance that they sustained together as a couple until the firing of their very last kiln.

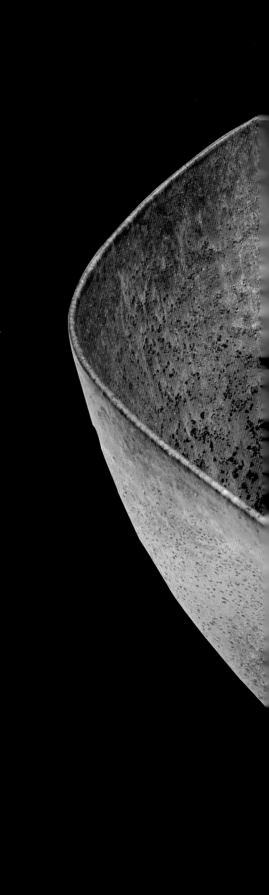

[1]All text excerpts in this section are from *Gertrud and Otto Natzler Ceramics: Catalog of the Collection of Mrs. Leonard M. Sperry,* © 1968 Museum Association/LACMA. Reprinted by permission.

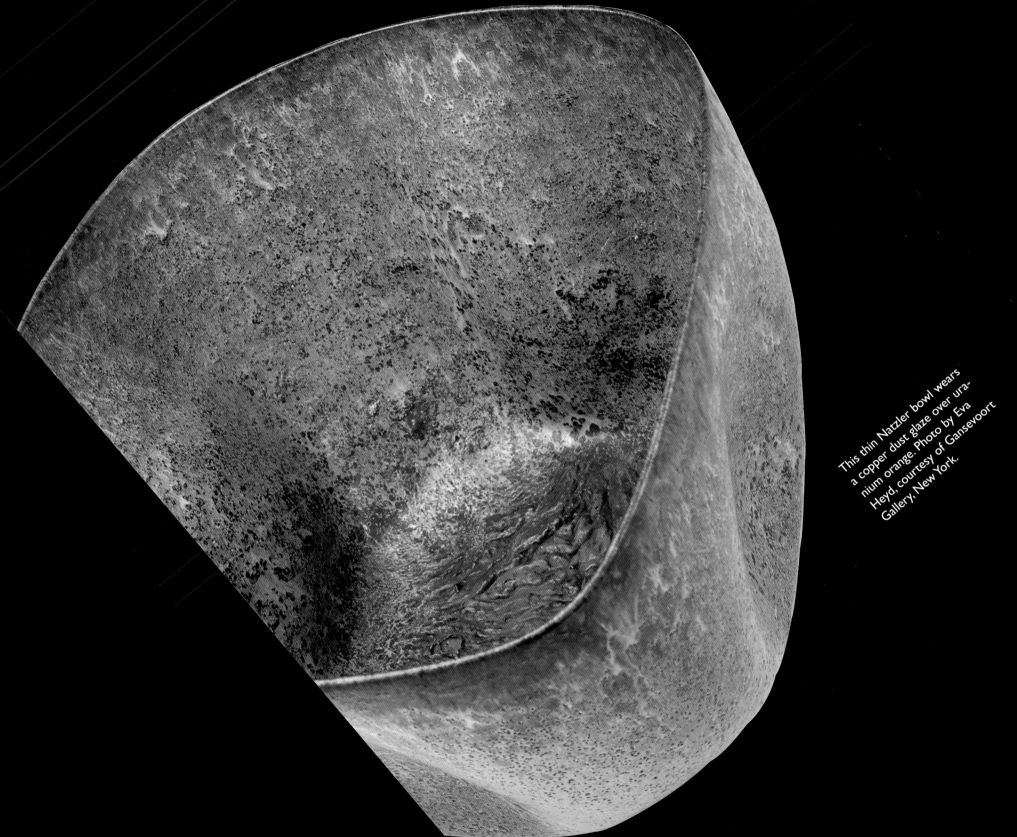

This thin Natzler bowl wears a copper dust glaze over uranium orange. Photo by Eva Heyd, courtesy of Gansevoort Gallery, New York.

Stoneware bowl by Edwin and Mary Scheier.
Photo courtesy of Gansevoort Gallery, New York.

The Scheiers

While Mary and Edwin Scheier are another husband-and-wife potting team, matrimony is about the only thing they have in common with the Natzlers and the Cabats. It wasn't just that their style of work was so vastly different from their contemporaries. In addition to the biblical and sometimes neoprimitive iconography that typified their work, their decorative techniques and glazes were also very much their own.

Their method of working together was unusual. Mary did most of the throwing at first, and Edwin did most of the decorating. Later on, when throwing became too taxing for Mary, Edwin did most of the throwing as well. Their respective styles were quite different. Edwin, for example, adopted a more narrative style, evolving into a statement of birth, fertility, and regeneration. He worked on a large, and occasionally massive, scale, with heavily tooled figural designs bulging out from under intense glazing. Mary's pieces were more traditional in that the crafting of her vessels was finer, with more emphasis on construction and less on decoration.

The Scheiers were mostly self-trained in the ceramic arts, having discovered clay in that serendipitous manner where one day the craft presents itself as an option and the next it becomes a life's work. Both had been employed by the Federal Arts Project and, though Edwin was from the Bronx in New York and Mary from Salem, Virginia, they met formally in Tennessee while doing fieldwork. It was curious happenstance that, years earlier, while Mary was visiting her aunt who lived in Greenwich Village in New York City, she ran into Edwin while walking through the Metropolitan Museum of Art.

There was little in their upbringing that suggested potting would be their career choices. Edwin, due to the death of his father while he was very young, endured a hardscrabble upbringing and was forced to find work at an early age. After knocking around in a number of occupations, including delivery boy and boat hand, he was introduced to the arts and crafts by a coworker.

Edwin eventually settled on puppeteering as a method of social satire. He studied for two weeks under a Sicilian teacher of some acclaim, Rimo Buffano, in a public works class. This led to his being hired in 1937 to work in New York State, where he traveled to Civic Conservation Corps camps.

Enjoying success in that position, he was next appointed a coordinator of the Federal Recreation Project, which allowed him to travel through much of the South. There, he conducted workshops in the arts and crafts, instructing recreation workers. The curriculum included puppeteering, weaving, and leather crafting, though, curiously, not potting.

His continued success culminated in his appointment as field supervisor for the southern states of the Federal Art Project in North Carolina, Virginia, and Kentucky. Here, he continued to organize classes in arts and crafts at federal centers. On one such junket to the Big Stone Gap and Abingdon art centers in western Virginia, he was reintroduced to the director of these centers, Mary Skinker Goldsmith.

Mary had taken a job with the Federal Art Project because she saw it as a continuation of her training in the arts. She was eventually appointed director of the Abingdon and Big Stone Gap centers. She had to improvise her modeling and painting classes, which reached hundreds of children, because there had been no local art programs prior to her arrival. She even ignored the segregationist tendencies of the area by including African American children in her programs.

Mary and Edwin were married in August 1937 and quit their jobs with the Federal Art Project for the more secure profession of traveling puppeteers. Theirs was an odd and circuitous route, leading back to the WPA in 1938, where Edwin was made director of the Anderson County Federal Art Center in Norris, Tennessee. They once again taught classes in metalsmithing, woodworking, and other crafts.

Two footed chalice vases, forms typical of the Scheiers' most popular work, are examples from the 1980s decorated with neoprimitive designs of men and fish. They measure twelve and sixteen inches in height, left to right, respectively.

These chalice vases (1980s) are typical of the Scheiers' later iconography and glazing. The desiccated black glazes are often augmented with brighter satin-matte finishes such as the blue used here. The metallic green finish is also a later innovation.

While there, they met Dr. Hewitt Wilson, the chairman of the Ceramics Engineering Department at Washington University. He was responsible for developing the Tennessee Valley Authority's capacity to create high-quality industrial ceramics. He was also responsible for introducing the Scheiers to potting, providing them with the basic facilities they would need to pursue the craft. Having been introduced to the ceramic arts, the Scheiers sought out local folk potters to teach them this new and exciting venture. They once again quit their positions with the WPA to strike out on their own. This time, however, they left to become potters and not puppeteers.

By chance, the young newlyweds found suitable clay in Glade Spring, Virginia, in 1939, where they improvised a studio and began their professional careers. They both produced mostly functional pottery in the folk tradition. They received more encouragement in 1940 when they were awarded a prestigious second place at the Ninth Annual Ceramic National Exhibition in Syracuse, New York. This was the most important juried ceramics competition in the United States and the two were quite surprised by their success. This finally led to their being offered teaching positions at the University of New Hampshire by David R. Campbell, director of the League of New Hampshire Arts and Crafts.

It was during this period, stretching from about 1940 to 1960, that the two created their most important and memorable work. Encouraged by the collegiate atmosphere and released from having to make a living by supporting themselves away from the arts, the Scheiers were free to explore their craft in a supportive environment. Much of what modern-day collectors treasure was made during this time.

Prior to 1940, the Scheiers were young in their art and busy developing the skills they had not yet mastered. After 1960, they explored other crafts and decorative arts, including weaving, painting, and wood sculpture. While they continued potting through the 1990s, it seems that the vitality and ingenuity that marked their first two decades at the wheel eventually cooled into the repetition of earlier themes and techniques.

Nevertheless, their work during the 1940s and '50s was exemplary in every way. The Scheiers were technically proficient, as evidenced by the masterful wheel-turned pots they both produced. Their shape selection was anything but traditional and their subject matter compelling, even daring. While they produced their share of simply thrown vessels with only glaze and/or rudimentary brushed designs as decoration, they are remembered more for the allegorical biblical and fertility scenes they favored.

Many of their decorated vessels and chargers have similar themes, with alternating fish and pregnant women etched or modeled into the surface. Many of the fertility scenes show developed fetuses in the wombs of the women. Similarly, there are examples with men inside the bellies of fish. These designs often become parts of larger designs, where the decoration first appears to be perhaps men and fish, and then, upon closer scrutiny, the entire vase is a large face with the subordinate design serving as eyes.

Another huge vessel appears at first to be an African tribal-influenced oval face standing on a flaring pedestal. Its "nose" is, in fact, a strategically placed fetus in a large womb. Pieces such as these were certainly daring for their time and are startlingly powerful even today. Matched with their stark glazes, often metallic, these are more than just unusual because their technical superiority remained so consistent over decades of production.

Another example of the Scheiers' ceramic mastery is their series of painterly chargers and discs. These are wall art more than ceramics, though the rich, baked-on colors and textures of the kiln invoke a feeling far different from any painting. These are often drawn with highly stylized designs of human figures, usually men, with etched-in sgraffito with faces and amorphous bodies. One such example, painted in black on a matte, apple-green bisque ground, looks like a 1940s psychedelic dream: precise, blunt, and commanding.

More common are biblical references, usually involving Eve, Adam, the serpent, and an apple. These figures are often entwined by the body of the snake, under a tree bearing a single fruit. The three are usually drawn in a flat style with little detailing, fitting into a scene that covers most of the surface of the vase or charger.

The Scheiers' undecorated ware is very similar to some of the Natzlers' flaring bowls, with small, rounded foot rings and thin walls. The glazes, though quite fine, never seem to match the intensity or variety of the Natzlers' work, however. They are usually smaller in scale, seldom measuring more than six inches in diameter.

This early charger (14
inches in diameter), dating to
the 1950s, is unusual in design and
technique. The abstracted body of a man is typical
of abstract expressionist work seen in American art
from this period. The design incorporates sgraffito
decoration (incised lines revealing the red clay
beneath) and enameling in bright colors.

What has evolved into the classic Scheier vessel is a *coupe*-shaped (goblet-shaped) vase on a cylindrical pedestal. The designs employed on these, often with blown-out faces on tooled bodies, repeat evenly around the vase's body. The glazes, in later years, became increasingly dark and the surfaces seem acid-etched or eaten, leaving a scarred appearance. Earlier examples tended to be more colorful in bright blues and greens.

There was a body of work produced in the 1950s that seems more utilitarian than decorative, though much of it bears simple painted designs. This was almost always produced out of soft red clay and covered with a white, tin-like glaze. Most

Feathers and faces decorate this *coupe*. Photo courtesy of Gansevoort Gallery, New York.

common are *coupe*-shaped mugs with pulled handles, delicately painted with animals in black or brown. While there is no denying the overall quality of this sort of ware, these pieces have none of the intensity or accomplishment of the Scheiers' more serious decorated work.

The Scheiers' scale was also very broad, and their better art ware was usually large by most standards. Chargers, for example, were usually no less than twelve or thirteen inches in diameter. While they made countless vases in all shapes and sizes, it is not uncommon to see vessels measuring over fifteen inches tall. During a show of their work at New York City's Fifty-50 Gallery in the early 1980s, some vessels measured nearly twenty-four inches in height. This is noteworthy because a potter has to move a great deal of clay around to bring a vase up so high. The Scheiers were well into their sixties at this point and this was no minor feat. It is all the more impressive considering the overall quality of their ware at this time and the diversity of the glazes they were still using.

It wasn't until the 1980s and '90s that their decorative ware became repetitive. While still respectable in quality, there seemed to be too many *coupe*-shaped vases with corroded black finishes showing blown-out men and fish. Gold luster used occasionally helps date these as newer works but doesn't add any enduring relevance to the pieces.

Describing what present-day collectors are looking for is a difficult task because, especially in their prime, the Scheiers' work was very diverse. Once again, the best pieces are usually large-footed vases or large circular chargers, decorated mostly in sgraffito. Yet some pieces were purely sculptural and others had sculpted designs on holloware bodies. Collectors have their work cut out for them: the Scheiers were always popular artists and their best work was often placed into collections when they were first made. As such, precious little of major importance is available at any given time. Usually, an old collection comes to market all at once and buyers are blessed with not only the chance to buy a superior cache of work but to glimpse, once again, the depth of the Scheiers' creativity at their peak.

Such pieces show other curious translations of their fertility and biblical scenes, but rendered in odd techniques or graced with surprising glaze combinations. One of the most refreshing things about the Scheiers is that their best work cannot be pinned down or categorized. While the Natzlers, for example, were always producing precise and beautiful pottery, one can "get" what they were trying to do, and even without having the chance to see all their work can envision what it might look like. The Scheiers, on the other hand, were endlessly creative and unpredictable. While Otto Natzler may never have ceased experimenting with glazes, the Scheiers never ceased experimenting with the idea of potting.

The fertility themes they so often chose might have been, on the surface, biblical references. But it seems more fitting that we view them as symbols of the fecundity of their creative minds.

Peter Voulkos

It is difficult to even begin to describe the importance of Peter Voulkos to twentieth-century decorative ceramics. He transcended the medium, helped elevate pottery to fine art, and in the process blazed the trail for those who followed him.

In spite of the vitality and growth of decorative ceramics in the United States in its brief seventy-five-year history before Voulkos, there was a prevailing bias that refused to recognize it as anything more than fine crafts. Ceramics were simply not appreciated in America the way, for example, oil paintings were. (It is interesting to note that in the Orient the opposite is true.) One of the ironies here is that, of all the arts, few offer better proof of the connection between the idea and the product than pottery.

Long before the time of Peter Voulkos, the Arts & Crafts potters understood that a work of art captured a moment, a spot of time defined by the object. Potting was an act of creation, of raising a ball of the lowest mud and, through the skill of the artisan, molding it into an *objet d'art*. While forming the pot, the vessel responds intimately to every touch, every idea of the artist. A push on its walls makes it shrink; a pull on them makes it expand. Fingers working up the sides of the vessel thin out the walls and increase its height. Clay is a supremely responsive medium, instantly conforming to immediate thought.

The more one reads about Voulkos's work and his methods, the more he seems a reincarnation of the Biloxi master George Ohr. Ohr, however, worked in a relative vacuum, producing extraordinary ware in a place and time when few cared, whereas Voulkos emerged as a leading figure on the cusp of our ceramic past, and heralded what it was soon to become.

An example of a Voulkos charger—a theme he would continue to repeat for several decades. The charger measures about fifteen inches in diameter.

Voulkos seemed at one with his craft. The essence of the ceramic arts, as Ohr said, was to remove oneself from the process and let God pot through the potter. While there seems little to clarify Voulkos's notions about the Almighty, those who have watched him work speak of the unity between him and his craft. And like Ohr before him, Voulkos introduced new techniques and ideas that revolutionized what people thought of the possibilities of clay. Where Ohr twisted, crinkled, folded, and dimpled his ware, Voulkos ripped at it, slashing wounds into his pieces, exposing the inside of the work as part of the idea. But unlike Ohr, who was mostly ridiculed during his time, Voulkos has become recognized as a master during his lifetime.

Peter Voulkos was born of Greek immigrant parents in Bozeman, Montana, in 1924. He graduated from high school in 1942 and soon began working for the Defense Department in Portland, Oregon, where he developed some of the skills he would use later as a sculptor.

He was soon drafted into the army to serve in World War II and, after being discharged in 1946, went on to college on the GI Bill. It was suggested by one of his superiors that he was not cut out to be a doctor or a lawyer and should focus on seeking a career requiring manual skills, such as an artist.

Peter Voulkos introduced new techniques and ideas that revolutionized the world of ceramics, as seen in this stoneware vase from 1960. Photo courtesy of Dane Cloutier, Laguna Niguel, California.

While at Montana State University in Bozeman, he studied painting with several abstract artists, including Robert de Weese. He chafed at taking a two-credit ceramics course until he was told he wouldn't be allowed to graduate without it. His teacher there was Frances Senska who would later become a renowned artist in her own right; though, at that time, she was just beginning as a professor. To his surprise, Voulkos immediately became enamored of working in clay. He even worked out a deal with the night watchman at the school, who would turn his head as Voulkos climbed through the basement window into the studio to continue his work until dawn.

Voulkos dug his own clays, as did Ohr, from a nearby river. This was critical, as it brought him intimately in touch with every aspect of the craft. The college allotted only twenty-five pounds of clay per semester and, considering the scale on which he worked, that didn't last a struggling student very long.

He continued to improve his skills and in 1950 won first place in the Syracuse Museum of Fine Arts National Ceramic Exhibition, still the most prestigious juried ceramics competition in America. Much of his work at this time was decorated by wax-inlaid line drawings. These usually appear as brown-painted decorations, sometimes figural but usually abstract, on gray or oatmeal grounds.

It is important to note that while Voulkos's earlier works have a "craftsy" look to them, they possessed a boldness uncommon among his peers. The color range of these early works was fairly limited, and the shapes tended towards globular jars with thinner, if not pinched, necks. But there was no denying the craftsmanship and the consistency of these pieces. There was a visual strength and a sureness of hand in Voulkos's work that, even in this phase of his development, separated him from his contemporaries.

Voulkos graduated in 1951 and continued on to pursue his master's degree in ceramics and stoneware at the California College of Arts and Crafts in Oakland; the subject of his master's thesis was lidded jars. Throughout these years, he continued to develop his throwing skills. According to his former teacher Senska, Voulkos was built like a "gorilla," and this innate power allowed him to keep his hands "perfectly still."

Voulkos was very fortunate to have both natural talent and influential people often crossing his path. In 1952, for example, he returned to Bozeman because he'd heard that a Helena, Montana, brick maker named Archie Bray Sr. was interested in building a pottery. In consort with another famous American ceramist, Rudy Autio, Voulkos reached an agreement with Bray in which they could use the facility if they helped build it and also assisted Bray in his factory, firing and glazing bricks. It was the first time in his life that he would have the opportunity to create his own working environment from scratch.

Later that same year, during a trip across the United States to assess the progress of the ceramic arts here, the Japanese master Shoji Hamada and the English master Bernard Leach visited the Archie Bray Foundation in Helena. During their stay, Voulkos would chauffer Hamada into the countryside to paint watercolors of the area. One serendipitous morning, as Hamada painted in watercolor, the work in progress froze on the paper, creating crystals of color. Hamada saw this as a welcome occurrence, impressing upon Voulkos how the accidental can be a positive element in art. While the vagaries of the kiln always resulted in inconsistency and surprises, this idea was inconsistent with the formality of the ceramic arts in America.

Soon, young potters from around the country heard about the work being done at Bray and arrived to study under Voulkos and Autio. In keeping with the spirit of the times, the curriculum was loose and spontaneous. This give-and-take was a radical departure from the rigid structure that previously existed in academia. While the decade after World War II was ripe for change of this sort, it was still slow in coming and not always welcomed when it did.

The next year, Voulkos was asked to teach a three-week course at Black Mountain College in Asheville, North Carolina. Asheville, a beautiful artists' colony in the foothills of the Smoky Mountains, had a history of creative thinking in the arts. The program at Black Mountain College was developed in part by Joseph Albers, who remained there from 1933 to 1949. Other important potters, including Warren Mackenzie and Daniel Rhodes, had also taught there. While at Black Mountain, Voulkos worked alongside artists of different disciplines, further enhancing his own skills and understanding of the arts.

After his brief stint at Black Mountain College was finished, he drove to New York City with a fellow artist, where they encountered the Abstract Expressionist artist Franz Kline and others in his circle. This marked another turning point in Voulkos's career, as their visually blunt ideas encouraged him to reevaluate his relationship with clay. It is important to remember that ceramics as a fine art was still a relatively young field in America and there was little to be learned from reading books. Trial and error and association with like-minded artists were the best schooling available.

In 1954, Voulkos took a teaching job at the Otis Institute in Los Angeles, where he once again had the joyous task of building a ceramics studio from the ground up. His assistant at that time was his first student, Paul Soldner, eventually to be regarded as an important potter in his own right. Similar to the Archie Bray Foundation, there was little division between student and teacher, and the atmosphere allowed for free thinking and experimentation. It would be helpful to think of the environment as a mix between the applied arts and playing jazz, where the exchange of ideas was like the spontaneous riffing of instrument breaks.

This stoneware vase from 1961 features brushed slip and colored glazes. Photo courtesy of Dane Cloutier, Laguna Niguel, California.

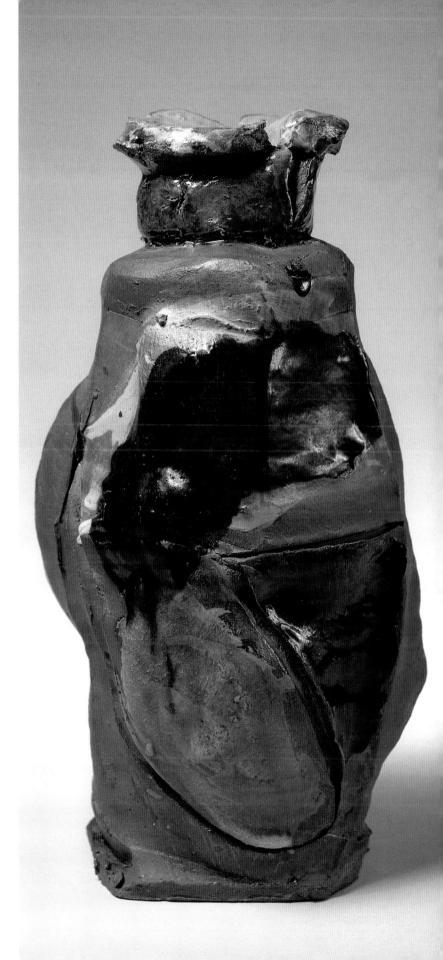

Voulkos had his first one-man show in 1956, held in Los Angeles at the Landau Gallery. There he introduced one of his newest creations, the rocking pot. This was dramatically different from anything seen in the ceramic arts anywhere in the world. The tall, hollow forms were pierced by ceramic rockers, like the struts of a rocking chair, redefining the interior and exterior space of the vessel. While revered by some of his peers, this was so extreme that even some in the potting establishment were incensed. (One of his former teachers cancelled her subscription to *Craft Horizons* in protest of an article they published extolling this new genius.)

It's been said that artists are the antennae of society. As Voulkos expanded the definition of potting, he ultimately offended the institution that hired him as a teacher. His work and his teaching methods were too controversial for these times. In 1959, after an object created by one of his students rankled an administrator, Voulkos was asked to resign. He was immediately appointed as an assistant professor at the University of California at Berkeley.

This middle period was Voulkos's most vital, though he continues to this day to make extraordinary pots. But while his skills grew throughout each decade, his work from the mid-1950s to mid-'60s was so different, so dramatic, that it resonated through the artistic community. For example,

This stoneware stack with pass-throughs is covered in black iron slip. Photo courtesy of Dane Cloutier, Laguna Niguel, California.

his decorative techniques for developing new surfaces incorporated implements such as nails, dentists' tools, pipes, and bottles. He seemed to attack the body of the vessel, exposing the inside, tearing the rims, slashing and punching until the final form was produced. By his own admission, each work was produced from within, the finished product a vague idea until the vessel coalesced at his fingertips.

Similarly, his sense of color was much in keeping with the Abstract Expressionists he admired. Such pigment, however, was used to accentuate the varied surfaces and textures of the pot, not merely to decorate it. Glazes were splashed on, slashed with a brush, or worked into the crevasses of the surface with the same brashness and vigor as the structural details they helped define.

Throughout this period, Voulkos worked exclusively with gas kilns. A gas kiln yields a relatively predictable result. Temperatures are relatively easy to control and the firing is "clean," in that there is little debris floating around the interior. It wasn't until the early 1980s that he switched to using a wood-fired kiln. A wood-fired kiln creates a wholly different environment, one in which it is difficult to keep the temperature at a consistent level, so the interior of the kiln is filled with floating ash that settles on the pottery. The ash imparts both color and texture to the ware. Also, placement of the ware in a wood kiln is of critical importance, as there are main and side chambers, each receiving different degrees of heat and a different flow of ash. Pieces would emerge with hot spots and odd colors and, in keeping with lessons learned from Hamada years earlier, Voulkos valued these as desirable happenstance.

The initial reaction of buyers and collectors to Voulkos's stacked pots was mixed. They didn't sell particularly well, and many of the surviving pieces from this period were those traded to fellow artists, who were among the first to recognize the importance of this work. This was less true of his sculptural work, which was more rare and of a more imposing scale. Such works have always commanded premium prices.

A broader market for Voulkos's work opened up around 1955 and continued through the mid-'60s, when he shifted his focus to bronze sculpture. When he returned to clay in 1968, the market was quite ready for him. This ushered in Voulkos's most successful period, both in terms of the work he created and the market for it. His plate series, which began in 1972, brought him widespread acceptance. He was also doing large stack forms at this time. While he continued to pot throughout these periods, most of his work was done during exhibitions and while teaching.

It is generally thought that Voulkos didn't reach his prime as a potter until the 1970s, though some of his best, most vital work was produced in the late 1950s and early '60s. Voulkos has never really had a bad period, though some of his work from the 1980s and early '90s seems less inspired. Nevertheless, as an artist in his eighth decade, he still produces masterpieces.

The increases in value for Voulkos's creations have been as extreme as his work. In the 1960s, some of his better chargers were selling for about $200 each. By the 1970s, they were valued between $1,500 and $2,000. In the 1980s, these same plates were bringing between $5,000 and $6,000. During the 1990s, the best of them were selling for in excess of $10,000. In the late 1980s, one of his pieces, a large sculptural pot, sold for more than $100,000.

His earliest work, though far from his most compelling, is excellent in quality and still inexpensively priced. Work from the early 1950s sells from about $1,500 to $10,000, depending on size and decoration.

It might be easier to understand Peter Voulkos's work by looking at the artware of the potters who followed him. In many ways, there are only two periods of decorative ceramics in the United States: before Voulkos and after him.

Porcelain pass-throughs and slip highlights make these stoneware plates dramatically different from other ceramics of the same era. Photos courtesy of Dane Cloutier, Laguna Niguel, California.

Two pear-shaped feelies, one in a lapis and malachite flambé, the other in a sky blue feelie finish, each measuring 4 inches tall.

Rose Cabat

In some ways, the decorative ware of Rose Cabat appears to fall short of the intensity or greatness of the other artists featured in this text. Judging her personality by the pots she created, you could easily be misled into thinking her a quiet and unassuming force.

Certainly, her work lacks the international impact of Peter Voulkos, Maija Grotell, or even the Natzlers, whose ceramic masterpieces transformed the very meaning of midcentury decorative ceramics. This is true not only in regards to the pottery each created but, in the cases of Voulkos and Grotell, to the teaching and instruction they provided to a generation of pre- and postwar artists.

Though Rose Cabat, like Voulkos, worked in several styles until hitting her stride with her trademark "feelie" vases, she is primarily respected for developing one type of ware throughout her tenure as a ceramic artist. Fortunately for her and for collectors of midcentury ceramics, this style was favored by the buying public—easy on the eyes and ultimately quite affordable. Artists like Voulkos, on the other hand, were challenging in every way, and Voulkos's work was never inexpensive enough to become commercially popular, even if his aggressive style could have enjoyed a wider appeal.

Yet Rose Cabat seems the perfect artist to close this discussion because her work embodies a most important segment of midcentury decorative ceramics. Her vision is personal, exceptionally refined through relentless experimentation, and her art ultimately affordable. A generous evaluation would confirm that she distinguished herself by bringing beauty and craftsmanship into the realm of the discerning collector with average means.

Rose and Erni Cabat were a husband-and-wife artist team. Unlike the Natzlers and the Scheiers, their ceramic work evolved to become mostly Rose's expression. While Erni, a graphic artist of some fame, was the first of the two to explore potting, he never took to clay in the way Rose did. Where Rose treated the vessel form as a whole object, Erni thought it more a canvas on which to paint his ideas.

This curious division between a husband and wife both involved in the arts seems even stranger because of Erni's continued glaze experimentation, in spite of his dwindling interest in things of clay. Throughout their lives together, he continued to be a tremendous help to Rose, first as an inspiration and later as her primary sales agent. Rose was, in fact, never as good as Erni in her drawing skills and this was, at least in part, his reason for encouraging her to pursue decorative ceramics.

In 1940, Erni studied under Vally Wieselthier, the well-known Wiener Werkstatte artist who, like so many of her peers, immigrated to the United States prior to World War II. While this may have done little but to convince Erni that ceramics were not his calling, it served the Cabats in that one day he brought home a lump of clay that Rose slab-built into her first vessel.

Erni further encouraged Rose by giving her a Christmas gift of enrollment at the Greenwich Settlement House in New York City around the same time that Maija Grotell taught at the nearby Henry Street Settlement House. One wonders at the extent of their curriculum since the development of Rose's wheel-throwing skills were self-directed while there. Whatever the case, her time at Greenwich House provided a foundation for her mastery of the wheel in the decades to come.

Rose and Erni worked together for a while, much in the fashion of the Natzlers, with Rose throwing pots and Erni developing a variety of relatively crude glazes. It's an expression of how young

An unusual "medallion" feelie covered with Cabat's trademark onion-skin flambé glaze sits next to a sky blue-and-green flambé feelie. Their heights are 4 and 7 inches, respectively.

Blue-and-brown-flambé pear-shaped vase, 6 inches tall.

Squat bulbous Cabat feelie vessel with a sky blue flambé, just 3 1/4 inches tall.

the field of art ceramics was in the United States that so much remained to be developed through experimentation. This, in spite of there already having been more than fifty years of growth in the decorative arts in this country.

As beautiful as much of America's art pottery had been, its success often ebbed and flowed depending on European and Eastern influences. This cut both ways, of course. Our potters relied primarily upon imported ideas and techniques, yet they learned to quickly evolve in their craft because they were not restrained by old-world themes and methodologies. Rose Cabat, like the Natzlers and Scheiers, began by establishing a foundation based on what had come before, and through their efforts, these artisans helped immeasurably to move the whole of decorative ceramics forward.

Like most postwar craft potters, Rose's evolution began with a fairly utilitarian strain of ware that focused on wind bells and the like. These paid some bills and served their purpose in helping to develop the skills she would eventually master. Hers was a journey that would take decades, however, and would lead her and Erni a long way from the Bronx, New York, streets on which the two first met as children.

When the Cabats moved to Tucson, Arizona, in 1942, they had no throwing wheel and were relatively short on supplies. Like the Scheiers, they devised a primitive throwing wheel from found machine parts. They were to remain in Tucson through Erni's death until today, where Rose still pursues her craft.

Erni first supplied Rose with red clay from a local brickyard. Rose primarily sculpted objects at that time until a proper throwing wheel could be secured. It became clear, though, that Rose was a potter-sculptor and Erni more of a painter-sculptor.

Their relationship slowly evolved into one where Erni became the businessman, learning to market Rose's work and, to a lesser extent, his own. It was at this time that Rose first developed her earlier "craft" ware, only to soon leave it behind in pursuit of a finer product. This progress is marked by her evolution from earthenware to stoneware and, finally, to high-fire porcelain.

Through years of work and experimentation, she eventually developed her feelie vases, a series of mostly small, globular vessels with trimmed foot rings and pinched, nipple-like closed rims, offered in a rainbow of fine, satiny glazes.

While the art ware Rose produced became more clearly her own, Erni still supported the effort by continuing his glaze experimentation. And this work, in turn, helped develop Rose's vision of her art.

Some have criticized Rose Cabat's ware as being repetitive and predictable, and, upon first blush, there may seem some basis for this. This is not an intellectual or visceral ceramic in the fashion of Peter Voulkos. Her work was, in many respects, diametrically opposed to Voulkos's jarring vessels.

The Arts & Crafts ideal of the late nineteenth and early twentieth century bespoke the need for "one artist/one piece." Reacting against the paucity of spirit in machine-made goods, the movement encouraged handmade objects for the sake of everyone involved. The craftsperson was enriched by the experience of creatorship, or seeing a piece through from start to finish. The object was imbued with the spirit of the craftsperson, as much birthed as crafted. And the end user enjoyed the sense of spirit and creativity embodied in the piece, benefiting from a relationship that could not be shared with a machined object, the offspring of a cold and heartless process.

This, of course, was the ideal, and, as English proponents such as William Morris eventually learned, handmade goods proved to be too expensive to produce, becoming mostly the acquisitions of the rich. One of the lessons learned after the movement made its journey here from Europe, around 1900, was that there were compromises to be made if the everyday person was to reap at least some of the benefits of this philosophy.

This bowl is covered with a feelie glaze, though it is not a typical feelie form.

This squat onion-skin feelie is finished with Cabat's typical pinched-nipple neck.

Where the British eschewed the use of machinery of any sort, the Americans accepted and eventually embraced it, as a partner to be held at arm's length, to relieve the craftsperson of some of the drudgery of the work. A case in point would be the use of power saws to bring down large pieces of timber and then reduce them to boards. Craftsmen could be spared the heavy work and left more time for the finer details of cabinetmaking. It seemed a reasonable evolution in the relationship between man and machine.

How this relates to Rose Cabat's work is that, by handcrafting smaller vases using an electric wheel, she was able to produce a large volume that would ensure her artwork broad distribution. What made this particularly significant, and assured her place in American decorative ceramics, is that amidst this output, she maintained integrity as an

Cabat's feelie glazes are as recognizable by the sound they make when handled as they are by their crisp, brilliant color. The squat emerald feelie has a pinched lapis neck.

artist, both personally and in her work. She provided for the distribution of her work in a way that historical greats such as Morris could never have imagined.

It is important to add here that her work was never intended to be souvenir ware. By its very nature, it is nonfunctional. The necks, for example, are too narrow for any flower. Instead, there seems in Cabat's work an intuitive understanding of the grounding capacity of the ceramic arts, much in the way a touchstone brings the bearer back to center.

It's long been an odd truth that, to center a blob of clay on a spinning wheel, the potter too must be centered. You must literally align the clay with your very midsection. If the mass is off-kilter, the wheel, once activated, can send it flying off. So, too, do we share that need for centeredness, so we don't fly off the wheel in our own ways. There is an ancient and allegorical lure to the ceramic arts, and a host of reasons why they're so much in favor among today's collectors.

It's difficult to say whether the success of Cabat's work depends more on her forms or the glazes covering them. Both work in tandem to create a sensual experience unlike other decorative ceramics. While she experimented with a number of forms and techniques (including the more typical craft-related flaring bowls and covered casseroles, with tooled decoration and the like), the bulbous feelie remains the most interesting. There are several variations:

● Balloon-shaped vases are the most common, where the pot is bulbous and round with a pinched top and short neck. The small rim of the neck is usually rough to the touch, as though it was torn, and often brown, regardless of the glaze she chose.

Because the clay on the necks is paper-thin, these often nick or chip over the years. It is sometimes difficult without magnification to determine if a rim was damaged after production, because they're sharp and uneven in any case.

Rose herself has expressed that her feelies need to communicate, through touch as much as appearance, the tactile facet of her craft. While there are feelie vases in other forms, the balloon shape seems the most successful in conveying her ideas.

These feelies are usually smallish, ranging from a few inches to over eight inches. Most, however, are three-and-a-half to five inches in height.

● Pear-shaped feelies are tapering vessels with rounded bottoms and small nipple-like rims. While they can appear in a variety of glazes, they often bear a greenish-brown finish much like the fruit they so closely resemble. They are taller on average than the balloon-shaped vases, and some reach nearly twelve inches in height.

● Straight-sided feelies are sausage-shaped vessels that also share the pinched nipple top, a trademark of this work. While larger than most balloon feelies, these were not made as tall as some of the larger pear-shaped examples, probably because the form makes them somewhat top-heavy.

● Other shapes were occasionally employed, such as larger flaring bowls. While sharing the exquisite glazing of the more typical globular vessels, these seldom share the same appeal.

Glazing

You can immediately determine a feelie glaze by its satin smoothness and general fineness. When you run your hand over a feelie glaze, it makes a soft scratching sound. And, simply put, you want to hold these because, in concert with their smooth organic forms, they are inviting to the touch.

While these pots work well in many ways, the handsome glazing in and of itself is simply beautiful. Some of the glazes Cabat employs are interesting because they are unique to her work alone; she tended to repeat a handful of glazes after about 1970, with most of the experimentation taking place in the '50s and '60s. Some of the most popular and successful are:

A soft mauve-glazed shouldered feelie.

A squat spherical onion feelie.

More common and less visually exciting is this
bulbous blue feelie with olive trails.

● Onion skin—Characterized by a silky finish in tones of brown, golden brown, cream, and light yellow, there are often streams of fine crystals running through the flambés. This is among Cabat's most subtle and beautiful finishes. Generally, the more successful of these are dark in color.

● Malachite—With a satin finish, this is actually a combination of two glazes, one a rich royal to midnight blue, the other a fine emerald green. The blue covers most of the vase's surface and the emerald green streaks unevenly from the top shoulder, ending in running drips. At its best, the green is medium dark to deep emerald, and engages the vase surface in a haphazardly controlled fashion.

● Apple green—Sometimes in satin finish, sometimes in a clear gloss, this is a handsome glaze but lacks the punch of some of her other finishes.

● Fruit skin—Usually a patchwork of soft greens and browns, like a partially ripened pear, this is often found on her tapering feelie vessels.

● Lavender—When used in combination with feathered pinks, one would immediately recognize a vessel coated with it as being from her hand. While less brilliant than some of her other glazes, it remains among her best.

● Mauve and cream—These are softer and more subtle than most of her finishes.

It is important to note that Cabat occasionally employed a decorative variation where she modeled a circular black medallion into the vessel wall, in stark contrast to the soft glazing on the rest of the vase.

Once again, Cabat's work offers the perfect counterpoint to her contemporary Peter Voulkos. Her pottery was as artistically accessible to the general public as his was challenging, as reasonably priced as his was expensive, and as available as his was scarce. Nevertheless, it sacrificed nothing in quality and expressed equally as much as the artists who created each.

Other Ceramists

Turn-of-the-Century Ware

An assortment of matte green ware by various turn-of-the-century makers, including Weller, Rookwood, and Teco.

Strong

Harris Strong was widely known for producing individually decorated, commercial-grade tile for use in buildings and hotels across America. These tiles depicting a New York cityscape are among his most desirable.

Wood

Beatrice Wood was known as the "Mama of Dada," as she was Marcel Duchamp's mistress in France. In America, she studied briefly under the Natzlers and went on to establish herself as a creative and prolific potter, working until she was more than 100 years old.

Ohr

This piece by George Ohr has a lovely symmetry of design that gives the vase a feminine sensuousness.

Modern
Studio
Furniture
in America

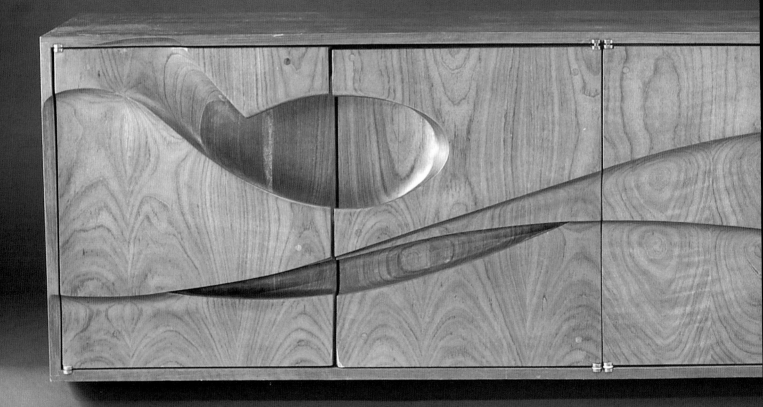

Sideboard

Michael Coffey – mid-1970s

This incredible sideboard with its Art Nouveau influences was produced by Michael Coffey for the Directional Furniture Company, where Coffey produced furniture throughout the mid-1970s. He replaced Paul Evans as the company's primary studio craftsman and designer. Coffey also worked with Vladimir Kagan, using Kagan's studio to help promote his work. The ceramic vase is by Maija Grotell.

A Personal Introduction
by John Sollo

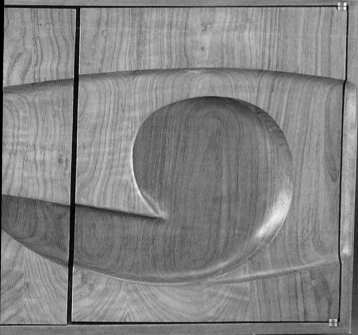

While walking the hallowed grounds of Brimfield in the mid-1980s and noticing the strong symmetrical lines of Stickley furniture, the gracefully organized curves of claw-footed Victorians and rows of elegant art pottery, a smallish chair leapt out of a shadowed corner, demanding my attention. It muscled the surrounding brown furniture to the periphery. This chair was the embodiment of anarchy, an attack of colors, a jumble of shapes and textures. It was a collection of unruly angles, seemingly at odds with the fundamental principles of gravity and physics. The chair screamed, "Look at me!" yet the lines were subtle, almost streamlined. It was covertly minimalistic.

The most amazing thing about it was that in so many ways it had the intimacy and feeling of private and personal expression. It was the perfect confluence of folk art with the cool lines and sophisticated design of modernism. It was a moment of epiphany for me. I asked the booth owner about the chair and he told me that it was made by a 1950s guy—a beatnik named Paul Evans.

83

I looked at this piece and felt at home with its contradictions, its ability to whisper and scream simultaneously, its violent collision with the mainstream. Yet I was overcome with its honesty and humility and its revelation of some basic truth about its maker. It was a very cool thing.

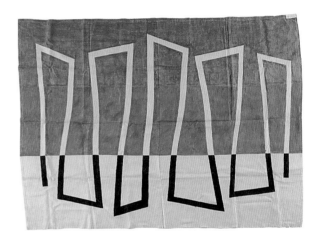

Tablecloth
Angelo Testa – ca. 1950

That day I became a modern collector. Although I enjoy and appreciate all types of modern design from the Bauhaus to Memphis, it is the rowdy rebellion of Paul Evans and Smokey Tunis, the integrity of George Nakashima and Phil Powell, and the integration of it all by Wharton Esherick that truly fascinate me.

The midcentury craftspeople were rebels amongst rebels, and that's really the history of the entire modern movement and the evolution of twentieth-century design. It is tale of doing battle with the status quo. This history is about artists, architects, and designers who reshaped, rethought,

Area Rug
Angelo Testa – mid-1950s

Testa's design influences are evident in this wool area rug. His association with Moholy Nagy at the Chicago School of Design gave him a firm grounding in Bauhaus principles.

and reinvented everything familiar in everyday life. They changed the way the world we live in looks and feels. They brought art to the ordinary, balancing and blending the ancient protagonists of form and function to create something new.

Deco Cabinet
Designer Unknown

This is a fantastic example of a Deco studio piece. Though the maker and date are lost to time and history, the piece demonstrates the freedom of style that is inherent to studio production.

Jazz Dining Room Chair
Designer Unknown
Some interesting designs have gone unclaimed—dates, designers and manufacturers have not been traceable to this point.

Each of the craftspeople written about here made a unique contribution to this evolution. They were completely free to tread outside of the boundaries. Their creativity was unstifled by corporate sponsorship and their thinking undiluted by academies or committees. More often than not, they worked alone, free to pursue their vision on their own terms. They were pioneers, though none of them would probably think of themselves that way.

Their contributions were many. They left us with good stories and great art. They resurrected and enhanced old techniques, developed new technologies, and experimented with new and radical materials. They developed business strategies that allowed people to actually make a living from their art. This part of their legacy can be seen in the work of Ron Arad, Marc Newson, and Albert Palley. But their biggest contribution wasn't their amazing craftsmanship or their unending innovation: it was their integration of emotional content with wood and metal. Their ability to elevate simple things such as chairs to an art form allows us to see parts of ourselves in the sleekness and power of their work.

Primal Throne Chair

Michael Shane – ca. 1970

Not all studio design is sleek. It is safe to assume that the owner of this funky design would be the only person on his or her block to have one. You have to love it.

Paul Evans

Paul Evans's work was an exploration, an adventure in possibility, a complete redefining of form. It was the perfect confluence of sculpture and furniture. Evans's art was an attack on the ordinary, an antidote for the mundane. It was a revolution of style and design. It was also a product of the times—a time of upheaval, of cultural realignment, of questioning. Paul Evans's craft captures and helps to define this period in American history. His work is a window through which one can reflect and reminisce.

Evans was born in Newton, Pennsylvania, in 1931 and demonstrated an aptitude for art and design at an early age. At nine years of age he had his first show in New York City.

His first exposure to the technologies that would later become the foundation of his craft—silversmithing, metallurgy, sculpture, and jewelry design—came while he attended the School for American Crafters in Rochester, New York.

In 1952, Evans's talents were acknowledged when he became the first American to win the prestigious Booth Fellowship. This scholarship allowed Evans to attend the Cranbrook Academy of Art in Bloomfield Hills, Michigan, and to develop the skills he would need to bring his art to fruition.

Metal Sculpture
Paul Evans

Paul Evans's most common sculptural form demonstrates his enthusiastic embrace of texture and color as artistic elements.

Upon completion of his studies, Evans moved to Sturbridge Village, Massachusetts, and worked as a silversmith, authentically reproducing colonial designs. He also experimented, operating under his own vision. His forms were expressive, using clean lines and a graceful balance to manifest a style reminiscent of Art Nouveau. This experimentation brought him his first commercial recognition and success. Evans sold designs to the Raymor Company and also attracted a wide following of European design firms that were eager to purchase his fresh and innovative work. Evans worked at Sturbridge Village until 1956, when his need to find a less-structured environment that would allow his art to mature pushed him on.

He moved to the rolling hills of Bucks County, Pennsylvania, and settled in the town of New Hope, which at the time was a thriving artist colony. It was alive with poets, painters, writers, and craftsmen. Its colorful swirl of beatniks and bohemians was a perfect environment for Evans. It seemed to invigorate and liberate his sense of vision, freeing him to create with the forceful passion inherent in his nature. Certainly, New Hope, with its liberal and creative air, became an important and supportive partner to Evans, encouraging him even in his most extreme and energetic designs.

Soon after arriving in New Hope, Paul Evans met the great woodworker Philip Lloyd Powell, a man who would become the most important creative mentor of Evans's life. Phil Powell had an established presence in New Hope: he was respected for his one-of-a-kind furniture, his impeccable

Lamp Table
Paul Evans/Philip Powel – late 1950s

This lamp table is a very early example of Evans and Powell's collaborative work. The metal radiating through the top of the table is pewter. The duo created an entire line of household accessories using this motif.

Sofa
Paul Evans – mid-1970s

This contoured sofa is an interesting example of Evans's later design efforts. It was referred to as the Hot Dog Sofa.

craftsmanship, and his integration of modern design with traditional and organic forms. The two men quickly became friends, with Powell convincing Evans that furniture design would not only be good for business but also would be a great canvas for Evans's prolific imagination. In 1956, Powell and Evans opened a joint studio in downtown New Hope, selling art furniture to weekenders visiting from New York and Philadelphia.

At this time, Evans began to develop what would become one of his signature styles: Sculpted Steel. Sculpted Steel was the perfect marriage of Evans's varied skills and experiences. It called on his extensive knowledge of metallurgy, jewelry design, and creative welding to produce furniture that had an explosive aesthetic impact. This impact was accomplished by organizing into collages a series of multicolored, multi-shaped boxes, each possessing a different sculptural element. When viewed from afar, they produced a powerful geometric tension, but from a closer perspective, they revealed an intricate mosaic of sophisticated sculpture. Evans integrated Sculpted Steel into many utilitarian forms, including coffee tables, room dividers, and especially buffets, thus providing a decorative and dramatic presence to otherwise ordinary household furniture.

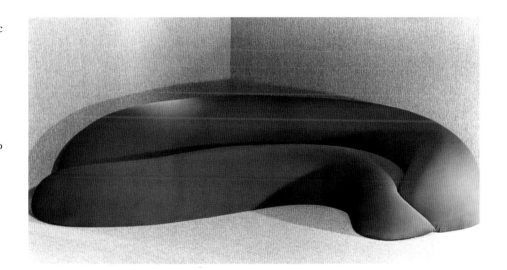

One of Evans's lasting contributions to the world of art furniture is his enthusiastic and pioneering embrace of new technology and his courageous use of revolutionary materials. Unlike his neighbor George Nakashima and his friend and mentor Phil Powell, who both shunned new technologies and nontraditional, nonorganic materials, Evans embraced technology, making it his own. This set Evans apart, giving his vision a level of chic modernity that was unparalleled at the time. Pushed by curiosity, he experimented endlessly—trying new welding techniques, new finishes and paints, acid and heat treatments. He tried countless combinations of metals, colors, and textures in an effort to perfect his craft.

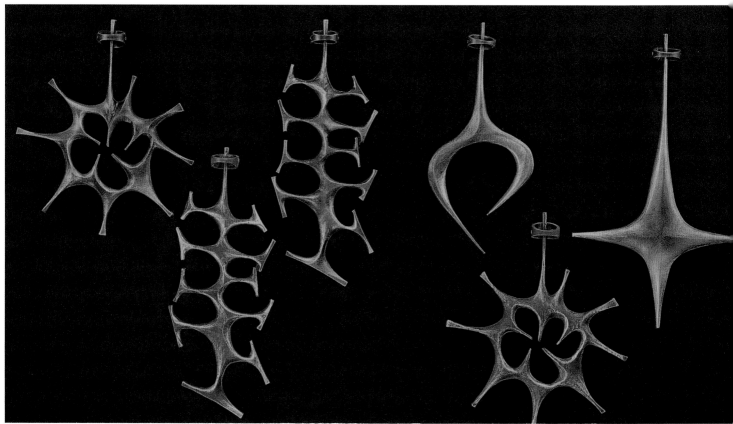

One goal of this endless experimentation was to find a method and a medium that would allow him to sculpt chairs, tables, and armoires freehand, much as a sculptor would work with clay. After years of failure and somewhat by accident, in 1964 Evans discovered a method that would fulfill this dream. He called it Sculpted Bronze.

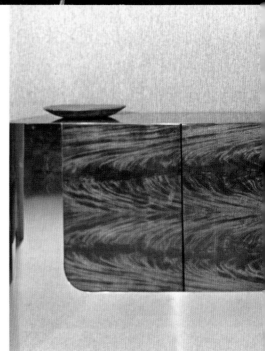

To create a piece of Sculpted Bronze, Evans would first construct a wooden frame and then coat the piece with a thick layer of epoxy resin. Into the resin he would sculpt various design elements, using a selection of tools and implements found around the shop or rescued from the junkyard. He repeated similar designs in many of his pieces, the most common being large circles, ellipses, and tread-like lines evoking a primitive feeling. After allowing the resin to dry, Evans would encase the piece with a layer of atomized bronze. The first forms

Evans made using this technique were office desks, but they lacked aesthetic cachet and met with only moderate enthusiasm. It wasn't until he applied this design technique to tables, chairs, buffets and his seminal work, the six-foot disk bar, that this style found success in the market.

With the addition of Sculpted Bronze to his line of furniture, Evans's work began to garner the attention of celebrities and those populating the glitzy New York mod and avant-garde scenes. It also came to the attention of the Directional Furniture Company, who in 1965 asked Evans to design and produce his signature styles for distribution in their showrooms. Their interest

Clockwise from top above, all photos courtesy of Dorsey Reading:

Sculpture-Front Buffet

One of Evans's most expressive and powerful creations was the sculpture-front buffet.

Paul Evans at America House; a magnificent Phil Powell cabinet hangs behind him.

Cabinet

This Alucobond-and-burl cabinet is an example of Evans's post-Directional production.

Door Knockers
Late 1950s

These doorknockers were made for the Raymor Company. Very few were produced.

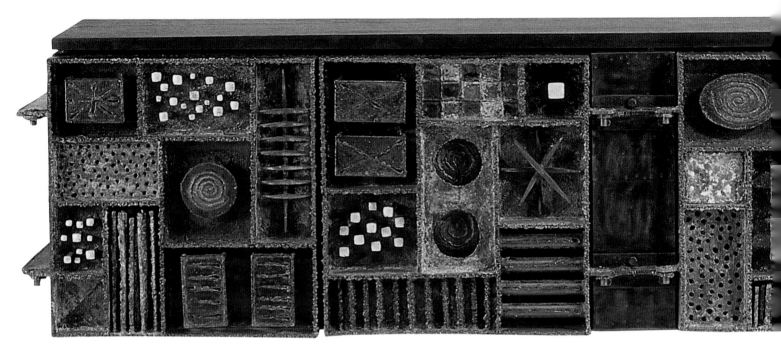

wasn't limited to Sculpted Bronze and Steel but also included Copper, Bronze and Pewter, a style using a patchwork motif of overlapping squares of copper and bronze with an applied overcoat of pewter. They were also interested in his Argente technique, which used shaded and textured aluminum to produce an incredible psychedelic effect. Evans readily accepted the offer, and a great collaboration of resources and abilities took place.

This relationship forever changed the scope of Evans's career. He could now enjoy a national and international marketing program of unparalleled sophistication. In addition to offering showrooms around the country and a robust contract and office business, Directional's significant following among top decorators and designers put Evans's work into America's wealthiest homes. This admittance to the highest echelons of the design world separated Paul Evans from his craftsmen colleagues and provided him with markets, capital, and a business infrastructure unimaginable to the average craftsman.

The importance of Paul Evans's relationship with Directional cannot be underestimated. If a person wanted to purchase a piece of Phil Powell or Wharton Esherick furniture, one had to search them out, travel to New Hope or

Sculpture-Front Buffet
Paul Evans – ca. 1970

All of Evans's furniture was unique, every piece designed to suit the artistic needs of a particular client.

Sculpture
Paul Evans – ca. 1965

Evans's sculptures are exceedingly rare and are aggressively sought by collectors.

Paul Evans and assistant Dorsey Reading building a Verdigris Copper door in the New Hope studio, ca. 1959. Photo courtesy Dorsey Reading.

Cabinet
Paul Evans – ca. 1962

A Verdigris Copper cabinet from the estate of puppeteer Shari Lewis.

Paoli, hope to find the craftsman at home, hope they had the time or inclination to do the work, and then wonder what the piece would cost. With Directional, a person could see Paul Evans's work in Seattle, Los Angeles, Dallas, or Chicago, know the price, and place an order.

As Evans's furniture gained national attention and sales grew, expanding his physical plant and production capabilities became necessary. In December 1969, Evans purchased a building in Plumsteadville, Pennsylvania, and moved his entire operation to this new location. He increased his workforce to between thirty-five and eighty people, depending on demand from Directional.

Paul Evans kept his New Hope studio open during this time, selling custom pieces that he had developed and refined over the years. From the studio he sold sculpture-front cabinets, steel-and-pipe lighting fixtures, complex storage units, and occasionally one of his sculptures. (Evans created sculptures throughout his career, but these pieces seemed to be more personal and were never produced in any quantity. It is thought that fewer than a hundred were built.) The work that came from the New Hope studio from the late '60s to the mid-'70s is considered to be Evans's finest and most innovative work.

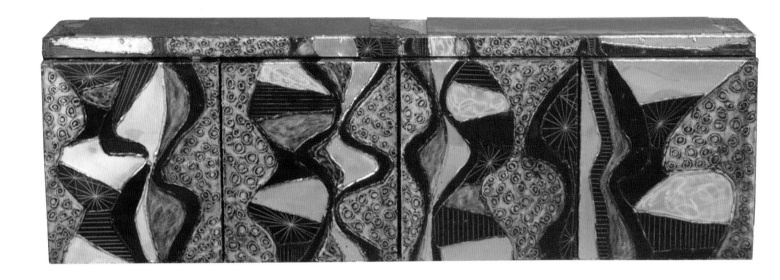

Argente Buffet
Paul Evans – ca. 1970

A spectacular example of one of Evans's rarest forms—Argente. In most of his buffets, his signature is found under the doors.

Sculpted-Bronze Buffet
Paul Evans – ca. 1968

Evans produced sculpted-bronze buffets in fairly large quantities. They were usually marketed through Directional Furniture Company.

After moving to the Plumsteadville facility, Evans began work on what would become his last and largest line of furniture for Directional, called Cityscape. It was reminiscent of Copper, Bronze, and Pewter but was smoother, with cool aggressive lines and a refined sophistication not evident in his earlier work. Gone was the far-out funk and unfettered search for aesthetic freedom, all replaced by an urbanized sleekness that possessed a decidedly techno feel. This complete metamorphosis of style is a credit to the depth of Evans's versatility. Becoming intensely focused on Cityscape, Evans virtually stopped the production of all other studio work. The Cityscape collection was produced in relatively large numbers throughout the 1970s. Then, in 1979, his relationship with Directional came to an abrupt end, due in large part to Paul Evans's desire to produce a line of radical furniture called Alucobond, made from bonded aluminum. He envisioned furniture much more extreme than anything he had done before. Evans was intrigued by the idea of adding motorized mechanisms that would animate furniture, bringing it to life. He dreamed of adding electronics to provide light and sound to chairs, beds, and bookshelves. He devised a plan so that entire rooms could be raised, lowered, or positioned to catch the best view of a particularly beautiful sunset. It was all too much for Directional, so the two parted ways.

Wall-Hung Cabinet

Paul Evans – ca. 1968

Due to the fumes produced while welding aluminum, very few examples of Argente aluminum were produced.

Paul Evans's relationship with Directional had been a symbiotic one. Evans received access to markets across the world, and Directional had an inspired inventory of cutting-edge art furniture, helping to preserve and advance its position in the fickle world of high-end furniture.

After leaving Directional, Evans opened a showroom at 306 East 61st Street in New York City. He designed and produced Alucobond and mechanized furniture, some of these creations having science fiction overtones. He built case goods that had electronically controlled doors and lights, shelves that could be rotated or adjusted by the push of a remote control button. He also sold a line of delicate coffee tables that possessed an elegance not seen in his previous work. He once again did freelance design work for various American and international companies.

The demands and pressures of a life dedicated to art and design were beginning to catch up with Evans. It had been a long road. He had gone from beat designer to international furniture craftsman, turning art into furniture. He had pioneered so many important techniques and materials. His efforts had led to the expansion and use of new techniques, materials, technologies, and market strategies. His career had been a success, and he had done all of it with good humor and charm. Some people didn't care for his work, but they couldn't help but like Paul. He was a true American character.

On March 6, 1987, Paul Evans packed his belongings and headed north to Martha's Vineyard to join his wife, to retire, slow down, and live the good life. On the morning of March 7, while watching the sunrise over the Atlantic, he suffered a fatal heart attack. His retirement lasted less than twenty-four hours.

Those who knew Evans weren't all that surprised. It was the creating that kept him going, his fanatical dedication to the next project, his endless doodling and his unlimited imagination. His friends knew that he was the architect of the life that ultimately killed him, but they also knew that he would have had it no other way. Phil Powell's eulogy summed it up best: "Paul Evans danced on the edge of the volcano."

Table Set
Paul Evans – ca. 1967
Sculpted Bronze was adapted to many different forms, including this end table/cocktail table set.

Disc Bar
Paul Evans – ca. 1967

This rare large disc bar with two semicircular sculpted-bronze
doors finished in a gold patina was built for distribution by
Directional. Fewer than two hundred were produced.

Paul Evans Collector's Addendum

Paul Evans was a creative and prolific furniture designer. In a career that spanned less than three decades, he designed, developed and successfully brought to the marketplace no fewer than seven distinctive and important furniture lines. In addition to these primary efforts, Evans's endless experimentation led to the production of hundreds of unique, limited-quantity pieces. Evans's artistic restlessness produced wonderful opportunities for today's collectors. However, organizing and identifying his various productions can be confusing. To help minimize the chaos, here is a brief outline of his major efforts.

● **COPPER, BRONZE and PEWTER** — This technique combines copper and bronze squares to form a symmetrical patchwork. Pewter is then splashed on for dramatic effect. Common forms are coffee and cocktail tables, mirrors and slate-topped shelves. Among the most rare examples is a cube club chair that swivels at the base and has an inset leather seat. This line is seldom signed or dated and was produced for both Directional and the Evans Studio. Prices range from $1,000 to $1,500 for common examples and from $4,000 to $5,000 for rare and one-of-a-kind pieces.

● **SCULPTED STEEL** — Produced from the mid-1950s through the mid-'70s, Sculpted Steel integrates the notion of severe geometric ornament with the enthusiasm and optimism of postwar design. This unlikely coupling produced a chic and powerful aesthetic. Common forms are coffee tables, lamps, and buffets. Rare forms include room dividers, wavy-front cabinets, and sculpture-front buffets. Sculpture fronts are often signed and dated. Look for signatures under buffet doors and under slate tops. Sculpted Steel is highly sought after by collectors and is considered by many to be Evans's finest works. This collector appreciation translates into strong prices for good pieces. Steel coffee tables and more-common forms can bring $2,000 to $3,000, while sculptured-front and wavy-front buffets often bring $7,000 to $9,000 and have brought as much as $16,000 at auction.

● **ARGENTE** — This line was produced from the mid-'60s into the early '70s. Argente is a line of welded aluminum that utilizes light and dark elements to produce a flowing pattern reminiscent of Art Nouveau. Because of difficulties encountered during production, very few pieces of Argente were ever completed. Common forms include cubes, pedestals and wall-hung buffets. Rare forms include highboy and lowboy dressers and full-length mirrors. Argente was primarily produced for Directional. Few pieces were sold through Evans's studio. It is seldom signed but very distinctive, and is highly sought after by collectors, with buffets bringing $4,000 to $6,000 and cubes in the $1,000 to $3,000 range.

● **SCULPTED BRONZE** — Production ran from the mid-'60s through the '70s. This is the style most associated with Paul Evans. It is made from atomized bronze and, in rare cases, atomized aluminum. Common forms include small tables, dining tables, chairs and buffets. The most rare and collectible example is the disc bar, considered by many to be Evans's most "over the top" design. Sculpted Bronze is usually signed and dated. The signature is often integrated into the overall design motif. Most Sculpted Bronze was sold through Directional. Because of larger production quantities, the Sculpted Bronze line offers collectors the opportunity to purchase Evans's work at prices that are often lower than what these pieces cost when originally purchased from Directional in the '60s. Coffee tables and small end tables bring $600 to $1,000 each. Disc bars usually sell for over $5,000. (A special note: Please see the design section on knockoffs, as there are many sculpted-front look-alikes in the marketplace.)

● **VERDIGRIS COPPER** — Production ran from the late '50s till the late '60s. This striking technique combines highly patinated copper with gold-leafed studs and long lines of unfinished copper loops. Evans reserved Verdigris Copper exclusively for cabinets. These pieces usually have bifold doors and patchwork bodies. They were sold primarily in Evans's New Hope studio. Very few of these extraordinary cabinets were produced and, when originally purchased from Evans, were extremely expensive. A major drawback of collecting Verdigris Copper is the size and weight of many of these examples. Some are so massive as to be impractical. Smaller examples, however, are well received by the collecting and decorating community. Prices range from $1,000 to $4,000.

● **SCULPTURES** — Evans produced sculptures between the mid-'50s and late '70s. Stylistically, these sculptures are difficult to categorize. They can be crafted using any number of techniques, including Sculpted Steel; Copper, Bronze and Pewter; Argente; or any combination of these styles. The most common sculpture form is the collage, which is a wall-hung adaptation of the sculpture-front buffet. Other than these collages, sculptures are exceptionally rare. It is believed that fewer than a hundred were ever produced. They are usually signed and were sold only from Evans's studio. These are of extreme interest to collectors and can bring very significant prices. They come up for sale so infrequently that it is difficult to establish a basis on which to draw market conclusions. Confirmed prices range from $6,000 to $7,000 for small pieces, and $15,000 to $20,000 for the larger and more dramatic examples.

● **CITYSCAPE** — Production ran during the early to late '70s. Cityscape is a patchwork of chrome and brass, reminiscent of Copper, Brass and Pewter. It was produced almost exclusively for Directional and is often signed. Cubes, small tables, and dining sets are very common, with streamlined desks and the faceted variation of this series being rare. Cityscape was produced in large quantities and was actively marketed by Directional's contract division. Except for the faceted variation of this style, collectors remain cool towards Cityscape. Prices range from the low hundreds for common pieces to multiple thousands for faceted pieces.

● **MULLIGAN STEW** — Evans was never bound by any single ideal or agenda and regularly created furniture that was quite contrary to his more-publicized styles. In 1976, Evans developed a line of cardboard furniture for college students. He worked with acrylics and aluminum. He produced a line of lamps made from exotic burls that brought to mind saguaro cactus. In the early '80s, one of his last design developments was a line of small occasional tables that were surprisingly delicate, demonstrating a sensitivity unique in Evans's portfolio.

Identifying Knockoffs

The only series of Evans furniture to be copied on any sort of commercial basis was the Sculptured Bronze line. With a little knowledge, it is easy to tell Evans's work from the fakes. Here are some tips:

● **MATERIALS** — Evans actually used atomized bronze in his furniture. This material has a smooth, cool feel to it and, if chipped, has a molten metal look. It will also get a verdigris look if exposed to moisture for any length of time. The fakes are made of a plaster composition and have a dull, chalky feel to them. If chipped or cracked (which the fakes have a tendency to do), the subsurface is a white plaster substance.

Most of Evans's bronze pieces have a green-gold hue. Because all of Evans's pieces were handmade and produced over a period of ten years, this color will be slightly different from piece to piece and year to year, but it is always green-gold. Imitations are often silver or sometimes dark maroon. The knockoffs also have applied patinas, usually consisting of multicolored coats of paint, while in Evans's work the color is inherent to the surface material.

● **USE OF SLATE** — This may be the easiest way to differentiate real from counterfeit. Evans always used real, natural-cleft Pennsylvania slate. The fakes almost always have faux slate, or wooden tops made to look like slate.

● **DESIGN** — This is another easy way to distinguish the chaff from the wheat. Evans never used flowers in his sculpting and very seldom used arrows or other nonabstract designs. Evans was a Cranbrook-trained artist and his work has a sophistication that the knockoffs simply don't have.

● **FORM** — The most copied forms are dining room sets. The sets consist of chairs with X bases and high backs usually upholstered in very bright colors. Buffets and glass-top tables are other often-appropriated pieces. An attempt was made to copy Evans's disc bar; however, the copies measure four feet across while the original measures six feet.

Philip Lloyd Powell

Philip Lloyd Powell was a midcentury bohemian, an artisan who ignored convention and convenience. He lived true to his beliefs, faithful to his own priorities. Powell's life was of his own design, crafted by his two great loves—travel and the production of studio furniture. Often Powell commingled these loves, creating forceful carvings to produce a sense of motion. Graceful swirls and arching sweeps created a momentum that challenged the observer, beckoning with the promise of adventure and a hint of magic. Powell also loved to incorporate found objects into his work. Trophies from his travels found their way into sideboards and cupboards—like Spratling silver bracelets as handles, oil paintings, and architectural elements—adding an air of mystery, a sense of drama, and a touch of the exotic. Each piece was a unique expression, all celebrations of Powell's extraordinary life.

New Hope Chair
Philip Powell

This particular example of a New Hope chair is a later version, possessing contoured back slats and a more refined sense of design than the earlier ones. It is estimated that fewer than thirty-six of these were ever built.

Phil Powell was born and raised in Philadelphia. At an early age, he demonstrated an aptitude for furniture design. In high school he crafted custom furniture for family and friends. This early work was based on traditional colonial designs but incorporated a modern sophistication that would become the hallmark of his later efforts.

Phil had planned a career in engineering and was considering various educational options when war intervened: in early 1941 he was drafted, trained as a weather forecaster, and assigned to the Eighth Army Air Corps. This assignment took him to England, where he was discharged in 1946. While stationed in England, Powell dreamed of living in a small Pennsylvania town nestled along the Delaware River—New Hope—where he had visited often as a child, antiquing or just enjoying a day out of the city. Thoughts of this place nurtured and sustained Powell's wartime hopes. It was a town of artists, writers, and painters, a place of dreamers and drifters, poetry and passion, a community where creativity flowed without fear or constraint. He might even be appreciated and be able to sell his work. It was a place of beret-wearing socialists, late-night cafes, and incredible art.

In 1947, Powell made his dream a reality. He purchased an acre of land and moved to New Hope. His homestead was on Highway 202, on the outskirts of town. It was a brushy, unimproved tract that the young Powell quickly began to develop. His original plan was to build a complex that would house a community of craftspeople—weavers, potters, painters, and furniture makers. The first job was to build a house. Never having built one before, he bought a how-to book and dived in. The house took shape slowly,

Phil Powell and Paul Evans in front of their New Hope studio. Photo courtesy of Dorsey Reading.

following Phil's own design, and it took on a decidedly modern feel. Large round rooms, magnificent views, a sunken fireplace, large showroom, and towering cupola all became dominant features of the home. During this time, Powell worked as an engineer to support himself and his ongoing building project, but he never lost sight of his desire to design and craft studio furniture.

In 1951, Powell began to utilize his strategic highway location to wean himself from his engineering day job. He did this by selling dead-stock Herman Miller and Knoll furniture and Georg Jensen products. He also became one of the leading American retailers of Noguchi lamps. A chance meeting with George Nakashima, another aspiring New Hope furniture maker, inspired Powell to begin developing his own product line. To this end, Nakashima began giving Powell chunks of walnut that were heavy with character and highly polished. Powell turned these pieces into a series of ultramodern lamps, somewhat reminiscent of Greta Grossman designs.

Later in 1951, Powell displayed some of his own work in his showroom. He offered the line of lamps built with Nakashima's wood, plus a line of slate-and-metal furniture that he produced in a local Bucks County shop. Much to his surprise, people began to buy his designs, passing up the Herman Miller and Noguchi in favor of his work. Powell was established.

Nineteen fifty-one also saw Powell design a line of build-it-yourself furniture for a local manufacturing company and teach classes at the Philadelphia School of Art. These

Phil Powell with a walnut and gold-leafed wall-hung cabinet. Photo courtesy of Dorsey Reading.

classes involved the integration of postwar modernism into craft, art, and architectural theory.

Powell moved his showroom to Mechanic Street in 1953. At that time, New Hope was awash with moneyed tourists, drawn by the town's artistic ambience, fine shops, and great play-house. Phil's showroom was only open on Saturday evenings, but that brought all the business he could handle, including custom orders. From his Saturday-night showroom, Powell sold coffee tables, lounge chairs, and dining tables, but the bulk of his production was chests of drawers. He made each one different, unique to every owner's whim. He carved elaborate patterns, utilizing and accenting the wood's natural properties. He added found objects, butterfly joints, and intricate dovetails, all acting to turn basic cabinet fronts into complex murals—wood tapestries alive with swirling currents of color and texture.

His client base was primarily young professionals, doctors, and lawyers, all trying to acquire a one-of-a-kind look. They were weary of colonial reproductions and paisley upholstery. Powell priced his furniture using the Dunbar Furniture Company as a guide. Coffee tables cost between $700 and $900, chairs between $300 and $750. Chests were $100 per linear foot and he couldn't keep up with demand.

During the early 1950s, Powell received occasional visits from an ambitious young man interested in a life of art and design. In 1955, this young man stopped by Powell's studio and the two struck a deal:

Powell would share his gallery and studio space with the newcomer, but they would keep separate books, profiting only from their own work. It was a great relationship that would forever change the face and nature of studio furniture in America. The young man's name was Paul Evans.

Evans had limited experience, mainly as a silversmith in Sturbridge Village, but Powell was a generous mentor, guiding and sharing business advice with Evans whenever possible. When Powell would sell a chest, Evans would make a pewter bowl or small sculpture for its top. When Powell required an exotic metal handle, Evans made one. Phil introduced Paul to the art circle of Bucks County and to the wealthy patrons hungry for studio furniture. Eventually, Phil Powell convinced Paul Evans to begin making and designing furniture of his own.

They often collaborated on pieces; for example, screens and storage units were often partnered projects. They jointly developed a line of wood-and-pewter accessories that they sold through the Raymor Company. They also combined pewter and wood in many pieces of furniture.

Probably more important was their cooperative design work. Powell and Evans did extensive interior decorating throughout the 1950s and '60s and were involved as advisors and suppliers to important interior designers across the country.

They also excelled as a team in salesmanship. They were a legendary two-man charm offensive, each searching for that key that would secure a sale. Even thirty or forty years later there are few who don't recall their experiences with Powell and Evans fondly and speak of the two of them with the highest regard.

During the early 1960s, Powell showed his work at America House, doing an exceptionally large and detailed arrangement. He also had several shows at the Museum of Contemporary Crafts, garnering critical praise and great national exposure. It soon became clear that Powell and Evans were moving in different directions. In 1966, they decided to split their showroom. Evans was embarking on a major project with the Directional Furniture Company, while Powell wanted to stay true to his original intent—his art and his craft.

Around this time, Phil traveled extensively, spending long periods of time in Spain, Sicily, Portugal, England, and Morocco. From each of these cultures he found inspiration. From the English he learned gold leafing. In Spain and Portugal he studied Moorish influences and the use of contrasting textures. In Sicily he developed a better sense of carving, especially the deep chip carving that shows up prominently in his work. From Morocco Powell developed an appreciation of doors and entryways, motivating him to create some of the most magnificent doors ever seen in modern architecture.

By 1976, the town of New Hope had changed. Gone were the throngs of free-spending tourists looking to rub

A classic deep-carved Powell cabinet is displayed at the America House circa 1958.

Below, Powell relaxes in one of his New Hope chairs. Photos courtesy of Dorsey Reading.

elbows with the artistic elite. They were replaced by middle-class day-trippers more interested in pizza and ice cream than daring counterculture furniture.

Deciding it was time for new adventures, Powell picked up and moved to Spain, staying there until 1979. Upon his return, he began once again making furniture with a distinctive postmodern look and feel. He made teacarts and lounge chairs, mirrors and dressers, mainly for old customers looking to round out their interiors or hungry for one more uniquely crafted piece from Phil.

Powell bought another property in New Hope in 1986 and promptly began to customize it. Included in this new location was a three-story tower where he now lives. It is adorned with an incredible Powell-designed door and spiral staircase that is not for the faint of heart. He still produces a few pieces of furniture, and participated recently in a show at the Michener Museum. He was, and remains, an integral part of the fabric of the Bucks County artisan movement. He stands out for his vision, vitality, and passion for pushing limits. His work and life have constantly evolved as Phil has looked for new ways to express his enthusiasm for living and art, and they are full of the energy that infuses everything that he touches. He is still a work in progress.

Philip Lloyd Powell
Collector's Addendum

A challenge that confronts those interested in collecting or decorating with Powell's work is that little of it is signed. It is often confused with the work of George Nakashima, Wendell Castle, Wharton Esherick, or Danish designers. There are, however, some telltale clues that can help collectors differentiate Powell's work. Here are a few:

● **LEAFING** — Phil Powell loved to incorporate gold, silver or aluminum leaf into his work. This becomes especially evident along table edges and exposed metal surfaces. Powell produced one series of furniture in which all surfaces were either silver-leafed or mirrored.

● **METAL** — Powell, due in large part to his association with Paul Evans, incorporated metal into his pieces. Metal could be used as supports, handles, or as decorative elements, and the metal could be gold-leafed, bronzed, or painted.

● **HINGES** — Piano hinges were often used in Powell's work. This is also a result of his association with Evans. Sometimes he would oxidize the hinges or give them a patina.

● **CARVING** — Unlike his neighbor, George Nakashima, Powell altered the wood with which he worked. He carved and sculpted it, enhancing it with his own vision.

● **FOUND OBJECTS** — Found objects were often incorporated into Powell's work. Marble, tile, chunks of bright-colored glass, jewelry, and even parts from Sicilian donkey carts are all possible indicators of a Powell piece.

● **BUTTERFLIES** — Powell regularly used butterflies as both a decorative element and structural support. His butterflies tend to be more dramatic than those of Nakashima or Esherick.

● **BREADBOARD ENDS** — Many of Powell's benches and dining tables have breadboard ends.

● **SLATE** — Powell was one of the few woodworkers to use slate as a tabletop, buffet surface, or cantilevered shelf. Usually he used natural-cleft Pennsylvania slate.

● **MARKETPLACE** — Powell produced fewer than a thousand pieces of furniture; therefore, his work is relatively scarce. Because of its high style, it's often kept in families from generation to generation, preventing its appearance in the marketplace. There are eager buyers out there and the market is quite strong. Pieces of particular interest are his chests, especially those that incorporate found items. Another collectible favorite is Powell's "New Hope" chair, which, in addition to having sleek, sophisticated lines, is extremely comfortable. Pieces that have a sense of humor or are particularly bold also capture the hearts and minds of Powell collectors. Quality examples of Powell furniture usually run in the $4,000 to $6,000 range. Chairs range from $1,500 to $2,500, depending on style and condition.

Bench Philip Powell

Powell, like his Bucks County neighbor George Nakashima, often used colonial designs for inspiration. This bench obviously borrows from period Windsor chairs but updates the style with modern accents.

Spiral Staircase
Wharton Esherick

One of the most stunning examples of organic design ever produced, this oak spiral staircase graces Esherick's Paoli studio. Photo courtesy of Wharton Esherick Museum.

Wharton Esherick

The art of Wharton Esherick is in many ways a distinctly American phenomenon. Like America, Esherick's genius was in his ability to take unrelated elements and combine them, creating something entirely new. His work was a process that commingled art and architecture, rurality and urbanity, simplicity and sophistication. It was an evolutionary process that mixed the power and mystery of nature with man's inherent need to create. The result was the elevation of craft to art, whittling to sculpture, and the production of some of the most challenging, beautiful and innovative furniture built in the twentieth century.

Esherick was born in Philadelphia on July 15, 1887. As a child, he demonstrated an aptitude and enthusiasm for drawing. He was able to pursue this passion by attending the Philadelphia School of Design and, later, the Pennsylvania Academy of Fine Art. Esherick never graduated, however. He found himself creatively confined by the academic nature and artistic intolerance of the Academy of Fine Art. Upon leaving the school, Esherick did land a couple of jobs in the art field—one as an illustrator for Philadelphia's two newspapers and the other as the resident artist for the Victor Talking Machine Company, across the river in Camden, New Jersey.

In 1912, Esherick, seeking to develop and define his artistic sense, moved to an isolated farmhouse in Paoli, Pennsylvania. There, surrounded by rolling wooded hills, he immersed himself in his painting. He also took time to observe and enjoy the intricacies of his wooded surroundings. He began to view nature as a potential partner and an ally in his art. Though it wouldn't be realized for thirty more years, the seeds of his radical designs and free-form art were developing every time he marveled at the strength and grace of the trees that populated his property.

Esherick moved to Fairhope, Alabama, in 1919, where he joined the faculty of the School for Organic Learning. Fairhope was a utopian colony, populated by artists, writers, poets, and craftspeople. It was in this unfettered and supportive environment that Esherick's vision for his creative future began to take form.

In an attempt to foster more interest in his paintings, he began to carve intricate and flowing designs into his picture frames, the designs often mirroring the subjects of the paintings. He also became interested in woodcuts, a popular and inexpensive method of producing high-quality but small-quantity print runs. Wharton Esherick's experimentation with woodcuts and his crafting of wooden frames at Fairhope would become the genesis of his furniture career.

Music Stand
Wharton Esherick – 1957

The cherry and walnut music stand is the embodiment of grace and emotion dancing to some imagined rhythm. Photo courtesy of Wharton Esherick Museum.

Desk and Stool
Wharton Esherick – 1927, 1929

This monumental carved-oak, drop-front desk built by Esherick in 1927 captures both the power and quirkiness of his work. Notice the vultures on the top two panels. The stool was built in 1929. Photo courtesy of Wharton Esherick Museum.

Esherick Studio

Without a doubt, Esherick's Paoli studio is his greatest achievement. He designed and crafted every aspect, from cutting boards and coffee mugs to the sagging roofline and free-form floorboards. Esherick's house and all of its eclectic contents have fortunately been preserved as a public museum. Photos courtesy of Wharton Esherick Museum.

Bok House

Wharton Esherick – 1937

One of Esherick's most important interiors was the home of Judge Curtis Bok. Seen here are the library fireplace surround, music room doors, and music room interior. Photo courtesy of Wharton Esherick Museum.

Esherick returned to Paoli in 1920 as a committed woodcut artist and a developing wood sculptor. He quickly turned his old barn into a studio and set back to work on his fine art. However, it was the power of his woodcuts and his growing collection of carved furniture that captured the eye of the local art elite. In 1924, he abandoned the idea of fine art and dedicated himself to the pursuit of furniture design and the production of woodcut illustrations.

High Stool/ Telephone Table
Wharton Esherick – 1969

A good portion of Esherick's production was dedicated to cupboards and storage spaces. Photo courtesy of Wharton Esherick Museum, photo by Richard DiLiberto.

The mid-1920s were a time of change, opportunity and exploration for Esherick. He received a number of commissions for his woodcuts, including the *Song of Solomon* and Walt Whitman's *Song of the Broad Axe* and *As I Watched the Plowman Plowing*, considered to contain some of Esherick's finest woodcuts. This work was hard-edged and extremely modern. It also expanded his reputation as an illustrator, successfully circulating his name through local and national art circles.

Sewing Cabinet
Wharton Esherick – 1933

Esherick's interpretation of a sewing cabinet. Photo courtesy of Wharton Esherick Museum.

At this time Esherick also began what would become a long relationship with the Hedgerow Theater, located in Moylan, Pennsylvania. He created sets, props, and promotional posters. There was a creative symbiosis between Esherick and the Hedgerow: the theater was the recipient of Esherick's vast store of creative talent and energy, while Esherick found inspiration in the many stories acted out on the stage. Some of his more interesting and playful pieces were produced for the theater.

In 1926, Wharton Esherick's furniture building, wood sculpting, and continued work as an illustrator produced too much activity for the small studio. To remedy this, he began to design and build a larger studio, located on the crest of Misery Ridge on his Paoli property. Esherick worked on this project for forty years. He dedicated his finest and most complete efforts to this studio, which was later to become his home. It became a showcase for both his artistic concepts and an inner view of Esherick, the man.

Every detail of the house, from its stone foundation to its switch plates and floorboards, were crafted by Esherick. Nothing was left unattended. He carved a stair rail from a mastodon tusk and coatracks in the likenesses of his fellow workers, and he built a host of gizmos and gadgets. He also built himself a bedroom that provided a soul-wrenching view of his world. His home was his greatest sculpture, a monument to his boundless imagination, his relentless and determined vision, and his subtle use of humor as an artistic device.

In addition to providing an emotional autobiography, Esherick's Paoli studio also demonstrated the range and complexities of his skills. It showed a mastery of architecture, woodworking, sculpture, furniture design, and carpentry, all executed with a sensitivity and respect for nature seldom seen.

Wharton Esherick's early furniture bears little resemblance to the sleek and sculpted pieces that he would craft later in his career. The early pieces were primitive, rough-hewn and heavy, drawing from the Arts & Crafts movement. In the early 1930s, Esherick turned to the larger design world for inspiration. He built pieces that displayed the extreme geometric tension that defined Cubism. He worked with the sleek but angular influence of Art Deco and showed an understanding of Art Nouveau and willingness to resurrect it for his work. He integrated Cubism and Deco into his interiors as well as his furniture.

One of his most successful interiors was for Judge Curtis Bok of Gulf Hills, Pennsylvania. For this effort, Esherick brought forth an entire spectrum of both technical skills and design inspiration. He designed and developed for the Boks a sweeping staircase that swirled through the house with a dominating, unapologetic confidence. Esherick provided the Boks with fireplaces, furniture, sculpture and archways. This effort was described as one of America's most outstanding domestic interiors by the *Encyclopedia Britannica*. Esherick's attention to detail and his ability to capture bits of the human experience in his wood sculpture took the Bok residence from good to great.

One example of Esherick's sense of detail and his ability to personalize any commission came from Judge Bok's unsuccessful attempt at running for district attorney. Just prior to the judge's leap into local politics, he had switched party affiliations. To help illustrate this political flexibility, Esherick added both donkey and elephant finials to the top of a ladder that was designed for the judge's library.

As the 1930s progressed, Wharton Esherick's work underwent an

Library Ladder
Wharton Esherick – 1969

A graceful and sensuous example of Esherick's "tree angles and tree forms" style, the elegant simplicity of this ladder helps demonstrate why Esherick is often considered one of America's most inspired furniture creators. Photo courtesy of Wharton Esherick Museum.

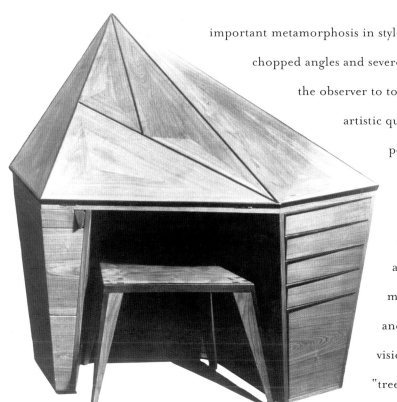

important metamorphosis in style. His vision became softer and more organic. The chopped angles and severe lines were replaced with sensuous curves that invited the observer to touch and caress. Esherick became more sensitive to the artistic qualities of his wood, learning to see and appreciate the potential in any given log. He learned to emphasize and enhance the inherent truth offered by the wood, mixing this understanding with his own genius to produce furniture that possessed both flow and lightness, qualities that made tabletops float and music stands dance. This furniture was fiercely modern and represented Esherick's expanding and maturing vision. This free-form furniture, or as Esherick called it, "tree angles and tree forms," represents his ultimate sovereignty of style, the complete spiritualization of his art form. He and his art had become indistinguishable.

Corner Desk and Stool
Wharton Esherick — 1931

This extreme design illustrates Esherick's commitment to cubism early in his career. The desk is black walnut with ebony trim. Photo courtesy of Wharton Esherick Museum.

Esherick showed his free-form furniture at the 1939 World's Fair in New York in collaboration with George Howe, an architect. His exhibition, "A Pennsylvania Hill House," won him national recognition from the critics. Esherick would call on his "tree angle and tree form" style for the rest of his career, utilizing it in his sculpture, interiors and furniture. It is the style most associated with him.

Esherick provided us with a large and extensive legacy. He kept the flame of handcrafted furniture alive during the machine age and provided inspiration to a new generation of woodworkers, including Sam Maloof, Phil Powell, and Wendell Castle. He helped to develop and introduce free-form furniture to the public. But his greatest gift may have been the power inherent in his works to transport us to some wooded Pennsylvania hilltop on a crisp fall day, where life is simple and the sky is blue.

Wharton Esherick Collector's Addendum

Wharton Esherick's furniture is rare and expensive. Even minor pieces that might otherwise escape notice command premium prices. Values begin at $2,500 to $4,000 for Esherick's three-legged stools, the only form that had any mass production. Middle-range examples like coffee tables, buffets and cabinets are commonly priced from $20,000 to $40,000, and his best pieces come to market so seldom that it is hard to gauge their value. Pieces that were "built-in" make up a large portion of Esherick's work. They tend to bring slightly less than freestanding furniture.

As with most other studio furniture, the most valuable examples of Esherick's work are those that showcase his intricate, meticulous craftsmanship or extreme designs. Interesting provenance (for example, being from a major commission) also adds value.

Esherick's woodcuts are also important to collectors, as they represent a significant period in his early career. They also provide a window into the inspiration for his furniture designs. Another advantage to collecting woodcuts is price. One does not have to be a tobacco trial lawyer to afford one. Most woodcuts sell for between $1,000 and $2,000.

Some identifying marks of an Esherick piece include:

● **SIGNATURES** — A large percentage of Wharton Esherick's work is signed and dated. Most of his free-standing furniture is signed but many cupboards and built-ins are not. Provenance then becomes important in identifying a piece.

● **CONSTRUCTION** — Wharton Esherick was a pragmatist when it came to the construction of his work. The carcasses of most of his larger case pieces were made of plywood. Drawers do not possess fancy or decorative dovetails and are also usually constructed of plywood. Often, Esherick would paint exposed plywood blue or salmon pink. In built-in pieces, the surface facing a wall might also be painted those same colors.

● **FINISHES** — Most of Wharton Esherick's finishes were produced with repeated coats of linseed oil rubbed in with fine-grit sandpaper. Like George Nakashima, Esherick considered the scarring of furniture surfaces by errant cigarettes or wet glasses to be a normal occurrence in the piece's evolution (an idea that is hard to explain to the average collector).

Corner Cabinet

This wonderful corner cabinet came from an important commission that Esherick did for a personal friend in Doylestown, Pennsylvania.

George Nakashima

Collectors, dealers and museums throughout the world covet George Nakashima's furniture. No single name in the realm of studio furniture is as recognized or revered.

George Nakashima's early life reads like an adventure novel. He was born in 1905 in Spokane, Washington, and as a young man spent days hiking and camping throughout the beautiful, rugged coastal mountains. As a teenager, he worked on a railroad gang and lived the life of a gandy dancer. He enjoyed some of the last vestiges of America's Old West.

In 1928, he received a scholarship to study in France. The following year, Nakashima earned a bachelor of arts in architecture from the University of Washington and was accepted into Harvard's post-graduate architectural program. However, Harvard did not appeal to Nakashima and he quickly applied and was accepted to MIT. In 1930, he graduated with a master's degree from their architecture school.

Buffet with China Closet
George Nakashima

This free-edged buffet with accompanying china closet exhibits a dynamic coupling of modern style with traditional Japanese.

Following his graduation, the young Nakashima landed a job with the Long Island State Park Commission doing architectural work and developing plans for parks, including the one at Montauk Point.

Writing Desk
George Nakashima – Late 1940s

This desk was crafted very early in Nakashima's career, probably in the late 1940s. The handle is constructed from bitterbrush, a species native to the American West. The wood was probably gathered by Nakashima during his internment in Idaho.

In 1933, George Nakashima embarked on a journey that would last the better part of the decade. This wandering would take him to some of the world's most beautiful places, expose him to the best in traditional and avant-garde art and architecture, and lead him to discover the moral, spiritual, and aesthetic truths that would sustain him and his art for the rest of his life. More than anything, it was these truths, this enlightenment experienced in his youthful journeys that provided the foundation for the extreme clarity evident in both Nakashima's personal life and his artistic expression.

Nakashima financed his trip by selling his beloved car and purchasing a round-the-world ticket aboard a tramp steamship. His first stop was Paris.

Paris in the early 1930s was awash with life and art. It was full of young rebels struggling to violate and expand the classic notions of art and literature. Nakashima eagerly joined the café culture—reading, working, and talking all night, and enjoying the creative current that flooded Paris. It was while immersed in the bohemian ambience of France that Nakashima began to question his commitment to architecture as a vocation, wondering about its absolute allegiance to technology and its dogmatic exclusion of freedom and joy for the object. He began to grow restless in Paris, and, pushed by the need to keep discovering and exploring, he found his way to Japan.

Upon his arrival, Nakashima stayed with relatives, learning the intricacies of Japanese society and culture. He took special interest in and developed a strong appreciation for the ancient designs and architecture of the Japanese. Nakashima took note of the attempts by Japanese craftsmen and artists to merge the old with the new. With this synthesis of time and style, the Japanese struggled to preserve and integrate their long-held notions of design integrity and traditional construction techniques with modern forms. Nakashima always sought this delicate balance throughout his career.

In 1934, Nakashima went to work for Antonin Raymond, an American architect working in Japan. Raymond had been instrumental in helping Frank Lloyd Wright build the Imperial Hotel and had his own office in Tokyo. Nakashima worked there for Raymond until 1937 when he volunteered to serve as the architectural supervisor for Raymond's firm during the construction of the SRI Auro Bindo Ashram at Pondicherry, India. He became a member of the ashram and began a life in search of divine consciousness.

His primary architectural mission at the ashram was to build the facility's dormitory. In addition to this, he also designed and crafted a large quantity of furniture. The furniture built at Pondicherry was constructed using primitive technologies and hand tools. This experience provided Nakashima with important and practical experience in wood sculpting and furniture design.

Nakashima reluctantly left the spiritual comfort of the ashram in 1939 and traveled to China. But intense fighting soon broke out between the Chinese and Japanese, forcing him back to Japan. Upon his return, he met Marian Okajima, an American of Japanese descent who was teaching there. They became engaged, returned to the U.S., and were married in Seattle in 1941. While there, Nakashima set up a small woodworking studio and executed his first private furniture commissions. These utilized the basic principles and aesthetic foundations that would be evident in all of his future design efforts.

Nakashima had traveled for eight years, seen the world, and had been exposed to its incredible capacities for both beauty and darkness. In 1941, evil and ignorance were on the march and would soon engulf the world of George Nakashima. For him, this introduction to institutional ignorance came a few months after the bombing of Pearl Harbor. Most Japanese Americans living along the West Coast were forcibly relocated, losing homes, businesses and possessions, and the Nakashimas were no exception. George and Marian Nakashima were interned at Camp Minidoka Relocation Center in

An example of chaotic burling. This amount of character adds tremendous value to any Nakashima form.

Hunt, Idaho. Nakashima did experience one stroke of good fortune there when he met a carpenter skilled in the ways of traditional Japanese carpentry. This man helped to instruct him in the proper use of hand tools and, more importantly, the idea that precision and patience must be partners in every phase of the woodworking process.

In 1943, Antonin Raymond, Nakashima's old employer, sponsored the Nakashima family's release from the internment camp. Nakashima joined Raymond at his farm in New Hope, Pennsylvania, but it didn't take long for Nakashima to decide that farm work was not for him. He returned instead to his passion—designing and crafting fine furniture.

Colonial forms heavily inspired Nakashima's early designs. Windsor chairs, harvest tables, and plank case goods were the genesis of his postwar production. However, though his designs were based on these forms, they were not strictly copies. Nakashima infused his work with a strong modern aesthetic. His production possessed a sleekness of line, lack of ornamentation, and a simplicity that, when integrated with colonial forms, produced a striking and powerful artistic effect. His work followed the pattern of what he had observed in Japan: the synthesis of traditional and modern, a combination that produced a look and feel that was unique.

Music Stand
George Nakashima
This music stand is one of two known to exist. It was built for Maestro Roland Fiori of New Hope, Pennsylvania, and fetched $25,000 at auction.

In 1946, Nakashima embarked on a short-lived collaboration with Knoll, Inc. Hans Knoll, founder and president, was assembling a team of top designers who would develop furniture to be manufactured and distributed by his company. Nakashima contributed several designs to this effort, the most important being the straight-backed chair—an adaptation of the classic Windsor chair—and a dowel-legged table that had sculpted breadboard ends inspired by colonial design as its most notable feature. Nakashima's involvement with Knoll increased his name recognition with professionals in the design field. This brought him a steady stream of capital that was vital to his operation and helped finance his own studio projects.

Around this time, Nakashima moved to Aquatong Road in New Hope, where he greatly expanded the scope of his studio business. He introduced several new forms, including the grass-seated chair and the slab coffee table. The free-edged slab table paid homage to organic naturalism and became the foundation of Nakashima's lifetime body of work.

Throughout the 1950s, Nakashima's business continued to expand. He was adept at self-promotion, and the expanding postwar middle and upper-middle classes were hungry for quality furniture. To meet this demand, Nakashima fleshed out his product line with desks, stacking tables, daybeds, side and end tables, and several other types of tables. In 1958, he designed a line of furniture to be produced by the Widdicomb Furniture Company of Grand Rapids, Michigan. This work relied heavily upon designs similar to the work that he was producing at New Hope, but it also incorporated elements and influences that were reminiscent of the furniture being developed in Denmark at the time.

Nakashima's work for Widdicomb tends to possess more radical angles, sharper, harsher lines, and a generally more modern feel than his studio work. In an important and uncharacteristic change for Nakashima, the Widdicomb furniture utilized veneers rather than solid boards, an effect that radically altered the aesthetic nature of this effort.

Nakashima's most dramatic and important leap in design development came between 1960 and 1961 with the introduction of the Conoid line, named for his Conoid studio. This effort demonstrates Nakashima's commitment to and understanding of the confluence of architecture and furniture development. The Conoid furniture group represents Nakashima's ultimate triumph—the successful integration of his own vision with his background as a trained architect. The drama, boldness and strength of the Conoid group set it apart from much of his other production. Included in the Conoid line are several examples considered to be some of Nakashima's most seminal works, including the Conoid Dining Table and Chair and probably his most recognizable form, the Conoid Bench.

This line provided Nakashima a viable platform from which to showcase his growing inventory and wide variety of decorative woods. The bulk of his day-to-day production was comprised of American black walnut; however, he also drew upon the unique features of many exotic woods to express his artistic intent. He often used European walnut, rosewood, English oak, redwood, East Indian laurel, cypress, and American oak.

Nakashima's understanding and appreciation of trees is legendary. No studio furniture maker developed a more sincere or deep-rooted relationship with his raw stock than did George Nakashima. His knowledge of wood transcended simple carpentry. He saw trees as portals into time, silent observers and magnificent witnesses to the fragile follies of

Conoid Dining Table
George Nakashima

This exceptional example of a Nakashima Conoid dining table with eastern burled top was bought at auction for $55,000.

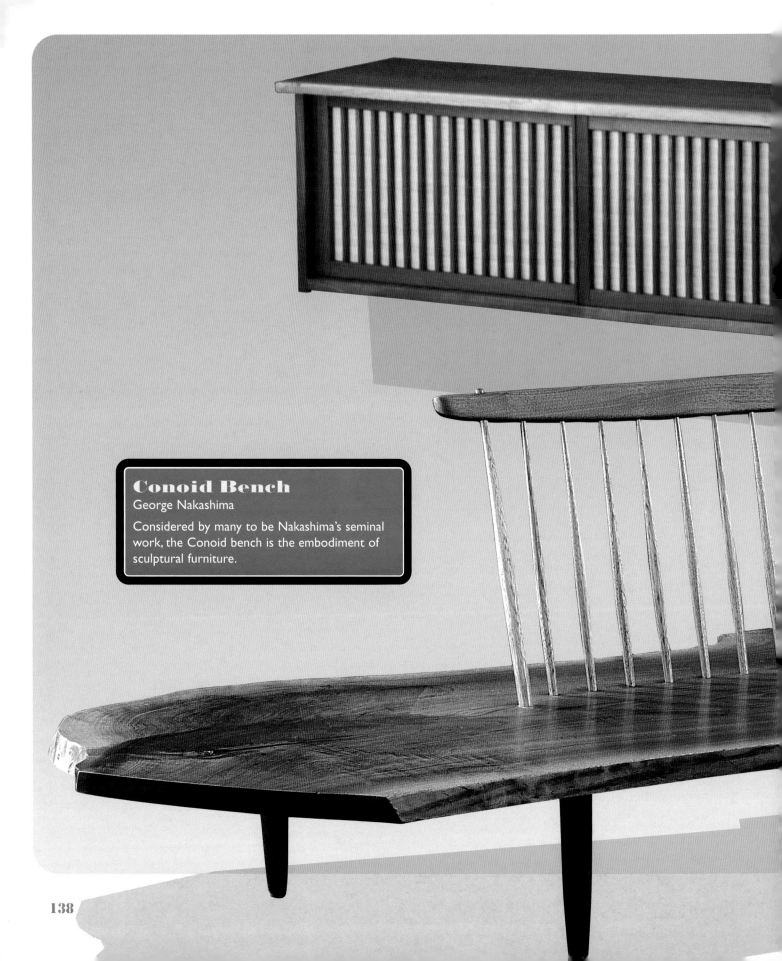

Conoid Bench
George Nakashima

Considered by many to be Nakashima's seminal work, the Conoid bench is the embodiment of sculptural furniture.

humans. Nakashima looked at wood with a religious reverence and tried to honor every piece of it. Feeling proud to resurrect and preserve the inherent majesty each great board possessed, Nakashima transformed this beauty into objects that would be admired and appreciated for generations to come, extending an immortality of sorts to the wood. He also possessed a keen awareness of how to best utilize every board to maximize its unique characteristics.

With the commercial success of his Conoid line and ever-growing access to great wood, Nakashima's business flourished. Throughout the 1960s, Nakashima continued to add innovative pieces to his inventory. In 1964, he developed the Kornblut Cabinet; in 1965, the Minguren I Table; and in 1968, the Minguren II Table. He also refined older designs, producing new looks by integrating their standard forms with exotic woods. Nakashima was also responsible for several important interior commissions, including Frenchman's Cove in Jamaica.

Nakashima's Harvard-trained architect daughter, Mira, joined him in the studio in the 1970s. Mira's collaboration with her father seemed to spark his designs to more radical conclusions and confrontational attitudes. Without question, her presence and contributions to her father's studio efforts were of great consequence.

In 1973, George Nakashima embarked on one of his most ambitious interior commissions—creating the furniture for Governor Nelson Rockefeller's Tarrytown, New York, home. Designed by Junzo Yoshimura, the house possessed a distinctly Japanese style and a sweeping view of the Hudson River Valley. Nakashima produced nearly two hundred pieces of furniture for this monumental project, including many unique variations of established designs. The Rockefeller commission was one of Nakashima's major accomplishments and a true testament to his design genius.

The legacy of George Nakashima is powerful and complex. It is impossible to speak to any of his clients without hearing wonderful stories of time spent with the woodworker, looking at designs and selecting just the right woods for each project, and the ambience of the Nakashima compound. But what becomes most obvious in these conversations is the tremendous feeling for Nakashima himself. He was a man of both spiritual and artistic clarity who sought truth in all of his endeavors. He had an abiding spirituality about him. Decades later, that spirit can still be felt as old customers reminisce about fall afternoons spent with him. This elegance of spirit is evident in his work as well, giving his craft a timeless simplicity.

Nakashima produced light fixtures (far left) for clients throughout his career, but they rarely come up for sale. When an example of Nakashima lighting is offered, it usually brings a substantial price. Nakashima produced an entire line of picture and mirror frames. Quite often these were crafted using exotic woods.

George Nakashima
Collector's Addendum

As with most studio furniture, the values of Nakashima's work extend over quite a range. Small occasional tables or single grass-seated or new chairs can bring as little as $700 to $1,000 each, while those expressing a particularly bold design aesthetic regularly command prices well into the five-figure range. Here are some important criteria for price differentiation of Nakashima furniture.

● **CONOID LINE** — The Conoid line prompts a particular passion for those interested in acquiring Nakashima's best work. This harmonization of architecture with furniture design holds an intrinsic appeal to most Nakashima collectors. Conoid forms usually outperform other examples at auction, usually by large margins. A single grass-seated chair may bring $700 to $1,000, while a Conoid chair can easily bring over $5,000. Fine examples of Frenchman's Cove or trestle tables often fetch $5,000 to $10,000 at auction, but a Conoid table can bring in excess of $20,000.

● **EXOTIC WOODS** — The incorporation of exotic woods can increase the value of any piece three- to fourfold. Rosewood is of particular value.

● **WILDWOOD** — Furniture examples that incorporate bold or dramatic wood selections are eagerly sought after by collectors. When the wood grain is more chaotic or expressive, higher values are realized on the furniture.

● **PROTOTYPES OR ONE-OF-A-KIND EXAMPLES** — Custom pieces or prototypes do tend to bring more money than most production pieces, but the value difference tends to be much less than in other areas of collecting. This is probably due to the large amount of custom and one-of-a-kind work that Nakashima produced.

● **BUTTERFLIES** — The use of butterfly joints as both a structural and decorative element is a George Nakashima hallmark. The inclusion of butterflies in any of his pieces adds value. In many instances their presence can increase the price by as much as 50 percent.

● **FREE EDGES** — Nakashima's use of free edges is another very important value criteria for collectors. Any example of Nakashima's work that utilizes free edges as a decorative component can bring twice as much as the same piece with square edges. The more radical the free edge, the more the value increases.

● **PROVENANCE** — Provenance can also be important in determining a piece's value. Examples from well-known commissions can certainly bring more money than pieces from those less publicized. Provenance can play an important part in authenticating Nakashima furniture. George Nakashima kept extensive records on his furniture production, including the style of furniture built, the wood used, the date produced, and the original customer's name and address. So if a collector purchases a piece of furniture knowing the original owner's name, he can verify the piece with the Nakashima office. As time goes on and pieces gravitate farther from their original owners, this method of authentication will become much more difficult. (Special Note: If you are currently interested in purchasing a piece of Nakashima furniture, it is highly recommended that you determine its origin. Serious collectors often tape the name of the original owner's name to the bottom of the piece.)

● **FINISHES** — Like Wharton Esherick, Nakashima used simple oil finishes on his furniture. He also, as did Esherick, considered normal wear to be part of any piece of furniture's individual history. (Nakashima called this the "kevinizing" process, in reference to his then-young son Kevin.) At this point in the evolution of studio furniture collecting, most collectors do not share this view about wear to furniture. Presently, pieces that have had their finishes touched up or have been entirely refinished have not seen those changes reflected in the price.

High Boy
George Nakashima
Nakashima's case goods usually feature tight dovetailing along the tops and minimally recessed handles, as evidenced in this walnut highboy.

Vladimir Kagan

Vladimir Kagan's synthesis of urban sophistication and organic naturalism led to the creation of furniture that challenged and expanded the very nature of the studio movement. His powerful interplay between rural and urban aesthetics demonstrates the most basic of studio conflicts—whether the craftsman should rely on design or material to provide an artistic impact. Kagan has balanced reverence for the material with mastery of design throughout his career, giving his work a look and feel unique in the studio world.

Born in Germany in 1927, Vladimir immigrated to the United States in 1938 with his family. His father, Illi Kagan, was both a master cabinetmaker and a devoted follower of Bauhaus design. Upon the family's arrival in America, the elder Kagan set up a woodworking shop in New York City, producing both his own designs and also constructing furniture for outside clients, including James Mont.

Kagan grew up in this environment, helping his father after school at the factory and learning the intricacies of cabinetry while developing his own sense of design priorities. While still in high school, Vladimir Kagan took classes from Dr. Müllen, an architect whose profound love of design inspired Kagan to develop a deep appreciation for both sculpture and architecture. From this relationship Kagan came to appreciate the complexities, the beauty, and the strength of bridges and buildings. This love for arches and spans, concrete and glass would become the foundation that Kagan returned to many times throughout the course of his furniture career. After high school Kagan studied architecture nights at Columbia while working in his father's factory during the day. This rigorous and demanding schedule immersed Kagan in the world he wanted to inhabit—the world of art, architecture, and studio furniture.

Chaise

Vladimir Kagan – 1958

This sexy chaise features sculpted
aluminum legs and is covered in
vibrant ultrasuede.

In 1947, through a connection with John Wannamaker, Kagan was commissioned to develop and design the interior of the delegates' lounge for the first United Nations headquarters in Lake Success, New York. For this interior, Kagan built cocktail tables, chairs, and case goods that possessed a rectilinear feel.

Kagan's career received another important boost when he was hired to work with Raymond Loewy on boat designs and in developing a series of shoe-store interiors with furniture and accents. This was a great experience that helped to form and hone Kagan's furniture sensibilities.

In 1949 Vladimir Kagan opened a shop on East 61st Street. His store was housed in an old Victorian building complete with fireplaces and an intrinsic charm. Here Kagan sold both his own studio-designed furniture and objects produced by other artists, including the ceramics of Louise Nevelson. Kagan's operation was a model of vertical business integration: he designed the furniture, his father did the actual production, and then Kagan sold the products in his own retail store.

Through a chance introduction in 1950, Kagan met Hugo Dreyfuss, a Swiss textile producer. The two formed a partnership and moved Kagan's store to a fashionable address on 57th Street. Here Kagan designed and sold furniture while Dreyfuss produced textiles. At this point Kagan's furniture was evolving into the organic curvilinear style that is now most associated with his work. His designs combined a graceful, enthusiastic, and avant-garde exterior with a powerful sense of architectural stability and substance, a contradiction that infused his furniture with a dichotomy of emotion and style.

Kagan sold his furniture to a "who's who" of both corporate and private clients, among them Marilyn Monroe, Gary Cooper, Walt Disney, General Electric, and Fairchild Aviation. Like the works of his contemporaries Phil Powell and Paul Evans, Kagan's furniture was very expensive. Chairs could cost $600 to $900 each and case goods were often $2,000 to $3,000 apiece.

Cubist Dining Group
Vladimir Kagan

Serene yet boldly architectural, the cubist dining group pairs chairs from the 1960s, upholstered in leather with American walnut frames, with the 2001 cubist dining table, which unites aluminum, walnut and glass.

In 1960 a slowdown in the economy led to the dissolution of the Kagan/Dreyfuss partnership. Kagan bought out Dreyfuss and reluctantly closed down the 57th Street store. He moved the showroom to the furniture factory run by his father on 83rd Street. He also began to expand the scope of his design effort, while continuing to produce his organic forms. Kagan began to experiment with harder-edged, more minimal designs. He also began to incorporate more radical materials, especially Lucite, which he used as a magical ingredient to give his creations the ability to float in space, unfettered by the power of gravity.

Throughout the 1960s Kagan continued to produce minimal furniture, with each design line becoming more aesthetically constricted than the previous one, until, finally, in the late '60s he could go no farther. He had taken the concept and production of minimal furniture to its farthest and most complete conclusion.

During the late 1960s and early '70s, Kagan's love of architecture and his fascination with buildings and bridges provided him with new inspiration. He created a line of glass-and-metal furniture somewhat reminiscent of the work of Le Corbusier and Mies van der Rohe. This line of constructionist furniture mimicked the skyline of New

York and provided Kagan with an entirely new look. Unfortunately, much of these efforts by Kagan fell victim to design pirates and soon had to be discontinued.

Because Kagan always had his own retail space in New York, he never relied on outside venues such as America House or other galleries to sell his material. His one attempt at nationwide marketing failed when a sagging economy forced the closure of numerous retail outlets, resulting in the loss of Kagan's consigned goods in various bankruptcy courts.

During the 1980s and into the '90s, Kagan did design work for several High Point firms. His first efforts were with Preview. Here Kagan mixed new designs with some of his classic ones, giving Preview access to the full range of his design resume. He then did work for Directional, becoming the most prolific and important member of their design stable. For Directional he produced a series of dining tables, dining chairs, some case goods, and a large selection of upholstered furniture. Kagan's relationship with Directional came to an end when the company was sold.

In the mid-'90s Kagan completely reorganized his design portfolio and re-released a slew of his old

Barrel Chairs and Ottoman
Vladimir Kagan

The clean, sensuous lines of Kagan's barrel design gives these pieces a timeless classic quality.

designs under the label Kagan Classics. In January 2000 Vladimir Kagan celebrated the arrival of the new millennium by releasing his New York Collection, an effort produced by Clubhouse Italia that will have worldwide distribution.

As interest in midcentury furniture grew throughout the '90s, Kagan's furniture began to be added to the permanent collections of many important museums, including the Cooper Hewitt, Vitra Design Museum, and the Metropolitan Museum of Art. Given museums' slow and somewhat haphazard patterns of collecting midcentury furniture, this inclusion of Kagan's work by mainstream institutions speaks volumes about his importance as a twentieth-century designer.

Probably no designer of studio furniture has been more prolific than Vladimir Kagan. There were years in which he would develop as many as one hundred new and unique designs—an amazing feat of design stamina. No studio furniture designer has withstood the test of time and the fickle whims of the American retail public with the grace and success of Vladimir Kagan.

Bilbao Coffee Tables
Vladimir Kagan

These free-form intertwining tables, finished in burnished silver, dance over the landscape of a living room.

Vladimir Kagan Collector's Addendum

Due to the sheer number of designs produced by Vladimir Kagan over his lifetime, and the vast differences in styles and forms he produced, his furniture has large variations in price. Small and more common pieces such as simple coffee tables or single chairs bring on average between $600 and $900, while middle-range goods such as dining chairs, dining tables, or case goods might easily bring $4,000 to $8,000 at auction.

Examples that are particularly expressive, especially ones that showcase his early curvilinear or organic style, can bring significant prices in the marketplace. This is especially true of his couches. His more minimal work from the 1960s has not attracted the attention of collectors the way his earlier productions have, and his 1970s Bauhaus-inspired furniture remains relatively untested in the marketplace.

Here are some helpful points in identifying Kagan's furniture:

● **SIGNATURES** — Throughout the 1960s into the early '70s Kagan signed some of his work using a branding iron, while other pieces were signed using cloth or paper labels. However, the bulk of his work is not signed. Collectors must rely on known forms or reliable provenances for authentication. (A special note: Kagan's work was pirated quite often, so beware.)

● **WOOD** — Kagan most often used walnut as his wood of choice but also utilized oak and, in some cases, mahogany.

● **UNIQUE DESIGNS** — While Kagan produced hundreds, if not thousands, of designs during the course of his career, he never built large quantities of any one example. Fewer than two hundred of his rocking chairs were ever built, with this form probably representing his most prolific effort.

● **CHAIRS** — Kagan produced more chairs than any other form.

Cork Screw Chairs
Vladimir Kagan – 1990s

Perhaps Kagan's best-known chair from the 1990s is the cork screw chair, seen here arranged in a pair for a conversational tête-à-tête.

Chair, Ottoman, Table, and Screen
Charles and Ray Eames

In many ways the work of Charles and Ray Eames has characterized our sense of midcentury design. The Eameses' innovative and daring use of materials, their examination and re-creation of common forms, and their creative vision make them important pioneers in the field. But they were not alone—all across America artists, craftsmen, architects and sculptors forged furniture that permanently and radically redefined the relationship between art, architecture, sculpture and furniture. This creative revolution was fueled in large part by the studio craftsmen.

Armchair
Otto Wagner

This is a rare example of Wagner's fine bentwood armchairs.

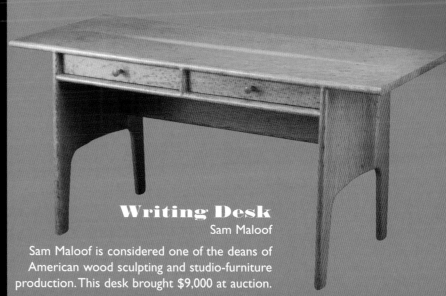

Writing Desk
Sam Maloof

Sam Maloof is considered one of the deans of American wood sculpting and studio-furniture production. This desk brought $9,000 at auction.

Wiggle Chair
Frank Gehry

Frank Gehry, best known as an architect, designed several lines of daring studio furniture. Most popular with collectors are his cardboard creations such as the classic wiggle chair.

Marshmallow Sofa
George Nelson

George Nelson's marshmallow sofa was designed by Irving Harper, a creative genius responsible for a large percentage of Nelson's designs.

Desk
Michael Bohn Clepper

This Memphis-inspired desk was handcrafted by Clepper.

Table
Karl Springer

This elegant table is a fine example of Karl Springer's work.

Porch Swing
Designer Unknown

Studio artists were not bound by convention, so interesting designs could be taken to their final conclusion, as seen in this porch swing.

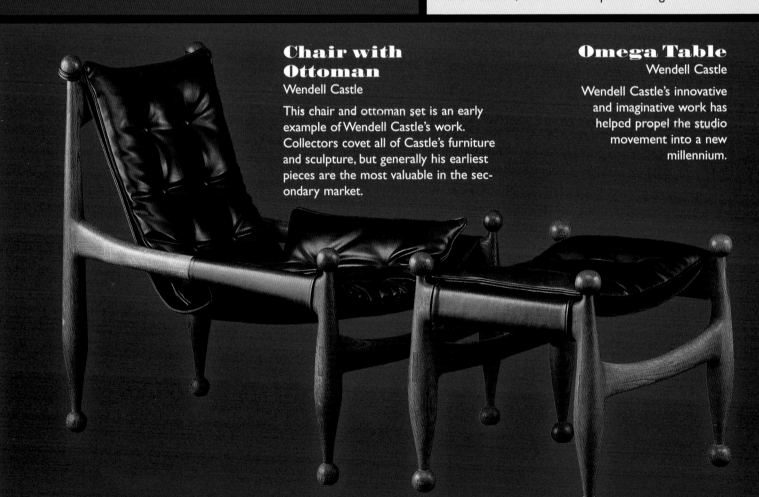

Chair with Ottoman
Wendell Castle

This chair and ottoman set is an early example of Wendell Castle's work. Collectors covet all of Castle's furniture and sculpture, but generally his earliest pieces are the most valuable in the secondary market.

Omega Table
Wendell Castle

Wendell Castle's innovative and imaginative work has helped propel the studio movement into a new millennium.

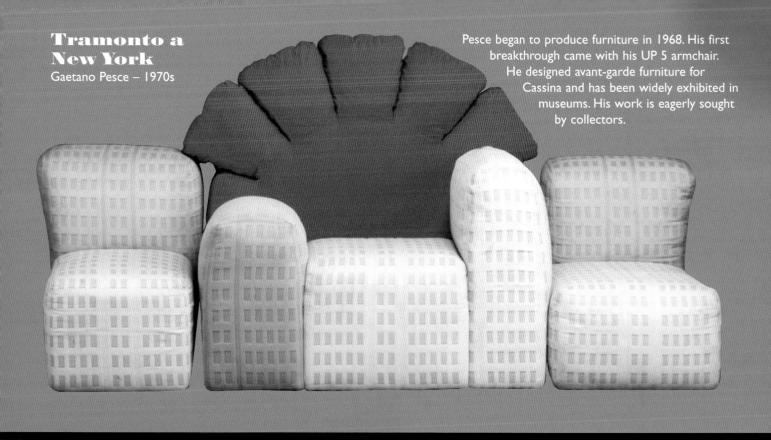

Tramonto a New York
Gaetano Pesce – 1970s

Pesce began to produce furniture in 1968. His first breakthrough came with his UP 5 armchair. He designed avant-garde furniture for Cassina and has been widely exhibited in museums. His work is eagerly sought by collectors.

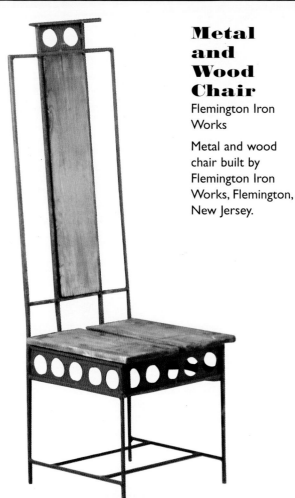

Metal and Wood Chair
Flemington Iron Works

Metal and wood chair built by Flemington Iron Works, Flemington, New Jersey.

Acknowledgments

These books provide useful information on studio pottery and furniture:

Aichele, K. Porter and Mansfield Bascom. *The Wharton Esherick Museum: Studio and Collection*. Paoli, Pennsylvania:
> Wharton Esherick Museum, 1977, reprinted 1984.

Clark, Garth and Margie Hughto. *A Century of Ceramics in the United States, 1878-1978*. New York: E. P. Dutton, 1979.

Komanecky, Michael. *American Potters: Mary and Edwin Scheier*. Manchester, New Hampshire: Currier Gallery of Art, 1993.

Marshall, Richard and Suzanne Foley. *Ceramic Sculpture: Six Artists*. New York: Whitney Museum of Art, 1981.

Nakashima, George. *The Soul of a Tree*. New York: Kodansha, 1981, 1988.

Natzler, Otto. *Gertrud and Otto Natzler Ceramics: Catalog of the Collection of Mrs. Leonard Sperry*. Los Angeles: Los Angeles
> County Museum of Art, 1968.

Ostergard, Derek E. *Full Circle: George Nakashima*. New York: The American Craft Council, 1989.

Perry, Barbara. *American Ceramics: The Collection of Everson Museum of Art*. New York: Rizzoli, 1989.

Quinn, Robert M. *Rose, Erni Cabat Retrospective, 1936-1986*. Tucson, Arizona: Tucson Museum of Arts, 1986.

I would like to thank Mark McDonald at Ganesvoort Gallery, Dane Cloutier, and Donald Davidoff. Thanks also to Robin Crawford for selling me my first piece of Natzler in 1977. And special thanks to Dr. Martin Eidelberg.

—David Rago

Many thanks to my beautiful wife, Nan, and my loving daughter, Megan; to Dorsey Reading, Phil Powell, Mira Nakashima, Rob Leonard and the wonderful folks at the Wharton Esherick Museum, Vladimir Kagan, Innkyung Hong, Amanda Jacobs, and Madge Baird.

—John Sollo

Selected Sources for Modern Collectibles

In Canada

Attica
1652 Granville St.
Halifax, Nova Scotia
B3J 1X4
(902) 423-2557
(902) 425-6824 fax

Design Manitoba
Donald & Wardlaw
101–326 Wardlaw Ave.
Winnipeg, Manitoba
R3L 0L6
(204) 453-2390

Design Manitoba Warehouse Store
92 Gomez (north of Higgins)
Winnipeg, Manitoba

In the USA

John Birch
Wyeth
315 Spring St.
New York, NY 10013
(212) 925-5278

Christie's Auctions
New York, NY

Dane Steven Cloutier
P.O. Box 6368
Laguna Niguel, CA 92607

Lawrence Converso
Converso
1932 S. Halsted
Chicago, IL 60608
(312) 666-6000

David Rago Modern Auctions
333 N Main St.
Lambertville, NJ 08530
(609) 397-9374
(609) 397-9377 fax
www.ragoarts.com

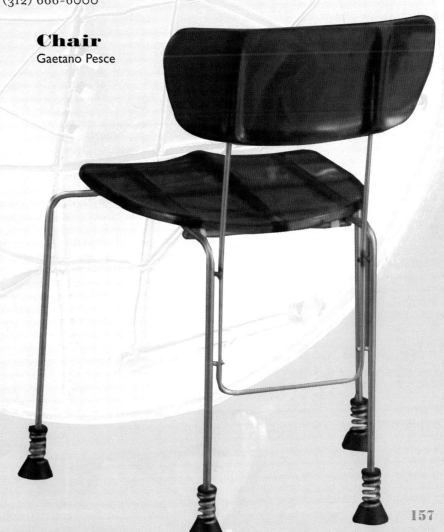

Chair
Gaetano Pesce

157

Anthony DeLorenzo, Inc.
956 Madison Ave.
New York, NY 10021
(212) 249-4119

Design Within Reach
(store and catalog)
455 Jackson St.
San Francisco, CA 94111
(800) 944-2233
(800) 846-0411
www.dwr.com
*New modern furniture from designers around
the world. Includes lines by Charles and Ray
Eames, Noguchi, Le Corbusier.*

Donna Schneier Fine Arts
910 Fifth Ave.
New York, NY 10021
(212) 472-9175

Elliott & Elliott
Dick and Diane Elliott
PO Box 751
Harbor Springs, MI 49740

Jack Feldman
Form & Function
95 Vandam St.
New York, NY 10013
(212) 414-1800

Rick Gallagher
280 Modern
280 Lafayette St.
New York, NY 10012
(212) 941-5825

Gansvoort Gallery
Mark McDonald
72 Gansevoort St.
New York, NY 10014
(212) 633-0555

Garth Clark Gallery
24 W. 57th St.
New York, NY 10019-3918

John's Resale Furnishings and Mid-Century Modern
891 N. Palm Canyon Dr.
Palm Springs, CA 92262
(760) 416-8876
Offering carefully selected mid-century classics as well as vintage modern.

Moderne Gallery
Bob Aibel
111 N. 3rd St.
Philadelphia, PA 19106
(215) 923-8536

Alan Moss
AMR Wholesale
436 Lafayette St.
New York, NY 10003
(212) 473-1310

Nakashima Studios
Mira Nakashima
1847 Aquetong Rd.
New Hope, PA 18938
(215) 862-2272
New pieces by George's daughter, who worked with him.

Jay Novak
Modernica
7366 Beverly Blvd.
Los Angeles, CA 90036
(213) 683-1963

Randy Roberts
1132 N. Speer
Denver, CO 80204
(303) 298-8432

Diane Rosenstein
Russell Simpson
8121 Melrose Ave.
Los Angeles, CA 90046
(323) 651-3992

Sotheby's Auctions
New York, NY

Think Modern
4820 International Blvd.
Oakland, CA 94601
(510) 532-1213
Restores and sells quality modern furniture, ceramics, glass and lighting, vintage 1930s through 1970s, including some by undiscovered designers.

Lin Weinberg Gallery
84 Wooster St.
New York, NY 10012
(212) 219-3022

Wexler Gallery
201 N. 3rd St.
Philadelphia, PA 19106
(215) 923-7030

Richard Wright
1140 W. Fulton
Chicago, IL 60607
(312) 563-0020
www.wright20.com

Partners Desk
Vladimir Kagan

Index of Artists

Lounge Chair and Coffee Table
James Mont